CULTURE SMART!
DOMINICAN REPUBLIC

Ginnie Bedggood and Ilana Benady

·K·U·P·E·R·A·R·D·

ISBN 978 1 85733 527 9
This book is also available as an e-book: eISBN 978 1 85733 564 4

British Library Cataloguing in Publication Data
A CIP catalogue entry for this book is available from the British Library

Copyright © 2010 Kuperard

First published in Great Britain 2010
by Kuperard, an imprint of Bravo Ltd
59 Hutton Grove, London N12 8DS
Tel: +44 (0) 20 8446 2440 Fax: +44 (0) 20 8446 2441
www.culturesmart.co.uk
Inquiries: sales@kuperard.co.uk

Distributed in the United States and Canada
by Random House Distribution Services
1745 Broadway, New York, NY 10019
Tel: +1 (212) 572-2844 Fax: +1 (212) 572-4961
Inquiries: csorders@randomhouse.com

Series Editor Geoffrey Chesler
Design Bobby Birchall

Printed in Malaysia

Cover image: *Victorian "gingerbread" style architecture (detail), Punta Cana Village.* © Pedro Guzmán: www.flickr.com/pedritoguzman. Also the photos on pages 31, 33, 54, 67, 80, 82, 85, 87, 105, 109, 110, 115, 119, 120 (bottom), 122, 123, 130, 132, and 164

Photograph on page 59 reproduced by permission of Angela Romero, and on page 81 by permission of Ginnie Bedggood

Images on these pages are reproduced under Creative Commons Attribution Share-Alike licenses 1.0, 2.0, 2.5, and 3.0: 14 © Niedźwiadek78 at pl.wikipedia; 18 © Fogster; 26 © Walter; 34 © Unai txola; 36 and 78 © Donpaolo; 45 © Dr. Eugen Lehle; 63 © Ponytail88 at en.wikipedia; 68 © www.hotelviewarea.com; 114 © Federico Izquierdo; and 124 © Captain-tucker. Images on the following pages are reproduced under Creative Commons Attribution 2.0 license: 60 © Lombinodr Alfonso Lomba; 116 © Joel Dinda from Mulliken, Michigan; and 117 © Daniel Lobo. Image on page 71 © iStockphoto.com

About the Authors

GINNIE BEDGGOOD graduated in History from Queen Mary College, University of London, undertook postgraduate studies at the LSE and Southampton University, and gained a Master's in Public and Social Administration from Brunel University. She worked as a probation officer in Soho in the 1960s and spent seventeen years as a social work academic at Buckinghamshire Chilterns University College before moving to the Dominican Republic. She has been living in Puerto Plata since 1992. Ginnie is the author of *Quisqueya: Mad Dogs and English Couple*, a narrative that charts her early adjustment to her new surroundings.

ILANA BENADY is a Gibraltarian who studied and lived in the UK for more than fifteen years, graduating in Politics and Social Anthropology from the University of Kent at Canterbury. Her work at the Oxfam headquarters in Oxford led her to the Dominican Republic in 1996. She settled there in 1999 and married Dominican photographer Pedro Guzmán. They and their son Lucas now live in Punta Cana on the east coast. Ilana is the coauthor of *Aunt Clara's Dominican Cookbook* and *Traditional Dominican Cookery*.

The Culture Smart! series is continuing to expand.
For further information and latest titles visit
www.culturesmartguides.com

The publishers would like to thank **CultureSmart!**Consulting for its help in researching and developing the concept for this series.

CultureSmart!Consulting creates tailor-made seminars and consultancy programs to meet a wide range of corporate, public-sector, and individual needs. Whether delivering courses on multicultural team building in the USA, preparing Chinese engineers for a posting in Europe, training call-center staff in India, or raising the awareness of police forces to the needs of diverse ethnic communities, it provides essential, practical, and powerful skills worldwide to an increasingly international workforce.

For details, visit www.culturesmartconsulting.com

CultureSmart!Consulting and **CultureSmart!** guides have both contributed to and featured regularly in the weekly travel program "Fast Track" on BBC World TV.

contents

contents

Map of Dominican Republic

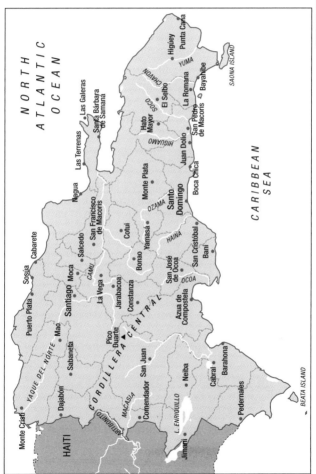

introduction

If you are looking for a country where everything works like clockwork, now might be a good time to close this book. The Dominican Republic has something for almost everyone, but not for obsessive perfectionists. If you can relax and go with the flow you will experience a land diverse in environment, a rich culture, a turbulent history, some infuriating idiosyncrasies, and a people whose friendliness is legendary. Flamboyant, resilient, irrepressible, generous, and headstrong, the Dominicans' psyche embodies their historical inheritance and reflects the diversity of their ethnicity and of the physical landscape itself.

The foreign visitor will find Dominican people extraordinarily helpful. This can often be misinterpreted as a quest for reward—and indeed, in some of the tourist areas, it sometimes will be. But what it is much more likely to signify is the natural Dominican curiosity about and interest in other people. Perhaps this stems from the particular mix of the Caribbean easygoing nature coupled with Latino verve and showmanship, but at any rate, visitors are not met with suspicion, despite the fact that historical experience could well have instilled a different reaction. Of course, helpfulness does not always mean that the task is achieved, but Dominicans will most definitely try.

This interest in people has its downside for some visitors, who can construe it as extreme nosiness. Likewise, the headstrong and hedonistic side of the Dominican personality can lead to irksome behavior such as littering or driving irresponsibly—and the irrepressible side can in turn lead to an abject apology, and a repetition of the same behavior the following day, when it has all been forgotten about!

Culture Smart! Dominican Republic offers a tantalizing insight into the country and its people, from the unspoiled coastline to the agricultural interior, to the imposing mountains, and the hamlets where time appears to have stood still. It then catapults you into the twenty-first century, taking you to the hustle and bustle of the large cities and the luxury coastal tourist resorts.

On this journey you will see both opulence and poverty, and you will witness contradictions that may make you feel uncomfortable. Showing you how Dominicans deal with those contradictions is one purpose of this book. Every aspect of Dominican life is touched by the key values of the importance of the family and the weight given to personal relationships and belief systems. This understanding of why people do the things they do, in the way they do them, underpins the practical advice offered on to how to behave in a Dominican home, or in social and work settings.

A book of this length can only be a taster, however, and inevitably will contain some generalizations. The main course arrives when you visit.

Key Facts

Official Name	Republica Dominicana (Dominican Republic)	
Capital City	Santo Domingo	
Major Cities	Santiago, San Pedro de Macoris, La Romana	
Geography	Occupies the eastern two-thirds of the island of Hispaniola, which it shares with Haiti.	Situated between the Caribbean Sea and the North Atlantic Ocean
Area	30,280 sq. miles (48,730 sq. km)	
Terrain	Diverse. Mountain ranges with tropical rain forests run east–west; arid semidesert plains in the southwest and northwest.	Highest point: Pico Duarte, 10,416 ft (3,175 m). Lowest point: Lago Enriquillo, -150 ft (-46 m)
Climate	Tropical maritime	Occasional hurricanes June–October
Currency	Dominican peso (RD$)	US $1= RD $ 36
Population	10.1 million (2010 estimate)	
Ethnic Makeup	Mixed 73%, white 16%, black 11%	
Age Structure	0–14 yrs: 31.8%; 15–64 yrs: 62.4%; 65 yrs and over: 5.8%	
Life Expectancy	Male: 70 years; female: 75.6 years	
Infant Mortality Rate	28 deaths per 1,000 live births; one month to 5 years: 30 per 1,000	
Language	Spanish	

Literacy Rate	Male: 88.8%; female: 89.5%	
Religion	95.2% Christian	Predominantly Catholic, although Evangelical Protestant Churches have made significant inroads in recent years
Government	Representative democracy. Bicameral National Congress consists of the Senate and the House of Representatives, elected every four years	The President is both chief of state and head of government and is elected every four years. Admin. divisions: 31 provinces and 1 National District
Media	Owned by large corporations, partially free press, active blogosphere	
English-language Media	DR1.com News, *Diario Libre* in English	
Electricity	110 volts, 60 Hz	Usually 2 flat-pronged plugs. Frequent outages
TV/Video	Uses the NTSC system	Some 46 stations are in the process of transferring to the digital spectrum via HD radio and HDTV.
Internet Domain	.do	
Telephone	International country codes: 1 809, 1 829, 1 849	
Time Zone	Atlantic UTC-4	GMT -4 (winter), GMT -5 (summer)

chapter one

LAND &
PEOPLE

GEOGRAPHY

Situated between Cuba and Puerto Rico, the
Dominican Republic occupies the eastern two-
thirds of the island of Hispaniola in the Greater
Antilles, with Haiti occupying the western
portion. It is the second-largest country in the
Caribbean after Cuba, and offers a diversity of
rain forests, fertile valleys, and cacti-strewn desert
regions cheek by jowl with four mountain ranges
and 1,000 miles (1,600 km) of coastline. It is
home to the tallest point in the Caribbean, Pico
Duarte at 10,400 feet (3,175 m), and the lowest,
Lago Enriquillo at 150 feet (40 m) below sea level.

What Is It Called? The DR vs. The Dominican

The Dominican Republic, the DR, La República,
or La República Dominicana are all acceptable by
way of nomenclature. The term "the Dominican"
will frequently be seen in publications unable to
differentiate between an adjective and a noun.

The country is larger than the Bahamas, Jamaica,
Puerto Rico, and the Virgin Islands combined,

and has some of the most beautiful and diverse topography in the Caribbean. Four mountain ranges running east to west display tropical rain forests and protect lush valleys, while in the southwest and northwest, arid semidesert plains can be found.

Environment

Hispaniola's geographical diversity and riches are reflected in its flora and fauna. It is the only Caribbean island with desert landscapes as well as tropical highland forests, wetlands, mangroves, and lowland dry forests. Dominican environmental law is comprehensive and forward-thinking, but as with many other areas of legislation the problems lie with interpretation, implementation, and enforcement. The southwestern part of the country especially is a bird-watchers' paradise. Wild mammals include the *hurón* (ferret), the *hutía* (similar to a hamster), and the solenodon, a rare, shrewlike creature that lives in the Cordillera Central and features on the endangered list.

Coastal Resorts

Although much of the DR's coastline remains unspoiled, readers will probably be familiar with the names of coastal tourism developments such as Puerto Plata, Sosúa, and Cabarete on the north coast and the Samaná peninsula on the northeast coast, with its virgin, white sand, palm-fringed beaches, hills of coconut palms, waterfalls, and small, traditional villages with bijou, pastel-colored wooden houses. The seaside resort towns of Las Terrenas and the quieter Las Galeras have recently seen development as the result of the new highway linking to Santo Domingo, the capital, and the opening of the international airport at El Catey. The present-day population of the peninsula is partly made up of the descendants of freed American slaves who settled there in the nineteenth century.

On the east coast, Punta Cana/Bávaro has been described as the ultimate Dominican success story. It was quite literally built from a barely populated wilderness; the founders were obliged to construct their own airstrip to bring tourists to their newly built hotels, because barring mules, donkeys, or a bone-shaking ride in a truck there was simply no other way of getting there. Today Punta Cana

International Airport is the DR's busiest. Nor is the area solely a tourist destination; many young Dominican professionals have moved there from the noise and bustle of Santo Domingo.

Continuing our coastal journey, the southeast is home to La Romana (Casa de Campo), Bayahibe, Boca Chica, and Juan Dolio. Inland from the coast, this is sugar-growing and cattle-ranching country; in sharp contrast to the more egalitarian and entrepreneurial vibe of the tourist areas, society here is semifeudal, with most of the land in the hands of a few wealthy landowners. Landless peasants survive on casual labor and subsistence farming, the starkest example of this being the sugar-growing areas—the cane-cutter settlements, or *bateyes*.

The Mountains

In the mountain range of the Cordillera Central, known as the Dominican Alps, the towns of Jarabacoa and Constanza base their economy on agriculture—with cooler-weather crops like strawberries, coffee, and pimento—and more recently on the development of adventure and ecotourism. Dictator Rafael Trujillo, who ruled the country between 1930 and 1961, imported about two

hundred Japanese families to work the fruit and vegetable fields around Constanza and improve the agricultural output of the region.

The Remote South

The southwest of the DR (known officially as "the south") is not an obvious first choice for most tourists visiting the country, but as the secret of its natural, relatively untouched state spreads, it has become increasingly popular with nature lovers and ecotourists. The Bahía de las Aguilas National Park contains some of the most attractive wild landscapes in the country. Unfortunately this has made it the subject of fierce conflicts between tourism developers who dream of building large hotels on the pristine white-sand coastline and conservationists determined to preserve its natural state. The main city, Barahona, was originally founded in 1802 by Haitian liberator Toussaint L'Ouverture as the French answer to Santo Domingo. The region is prone to natural disasters and suffered great material and human losses in recent hurricanes and tropical storms, such as Hurricane Georges in 1998 and tropical storms Noel and Olga in 2007. The town of Jimaní on the Haitian border was all but destroyed by mudslides in 2004, with heavy loss of life.

The Large Cities

Santo Domingo on the south coast is the capital of the DR and the oldest city in the New World. It is not your oft-imagined quaint, somniferous Caribbean capital. This noisy, vibrant, sprawling

metropolis has aspirations to being a mini New York City or Miami; it has certainly achieved this aspiration as far as traffic congestion is concerned! There are modern avenues, gleaming steel structures, and overpasses, but there are also many examples of crumbling infrastructure and poverty. Venture to Santo Domingo North to encounter the slum areas built by residents who moved from the countryside in search of employment and a better standard of living. Santo Domingo is the seat of government and a historical treasure trove in the Colonial Zone, as well as being the center of commerce and home to universities and some of the best hospitals and clinics in the DR.

Santiago is the second metropolis of the DR and is very definitely *not* a tourist town; its inhabitants have tended to consider themselves wealthier and harder working than those of the capital. A popular adage claims that Santiago is

where all the work gets done, but the capital is where the checks get signed. Set in the fertile Cibao Valley, Santiago has historically been the hub of the country's agricultural riches, and its millionaire families largely owe their fortunes to the sugar and tobacco grown nearby, as well as cattle farming.

CLIMATE

Temperatures in coastal regions range from a humid 77°F to 93°F (25°C to 34°C), with the temperature on the Caribbean south coast tending to be several degrees warmer than that of the Atlantic north and northeast coasts. In the mountain regions, "chillier" temperatures can be found—at times local newspaper reports refer to snow in the Cordillera Central mountain range, but on closer inspection this turns out to be frost. Even in the mountain cities like Jarabacoa and Constanza, the average temperature ranges from 66°F to 84°F (18°C to 28°C). Put it this way—it is not cold enough to grow Brussels sprouts in the DR.

Recent climatic changes have called into question the concept of the "rainy season," but the DR is in the hurricane belt. In the last forty-five years there have been ten hurricanes, or approximately one every four and a half years. Rain damage tends to be more pernicious than wind damage in the DR, and water damage and flooding can occur as much during a tropical storm as during a hurricane. Hurricane season starts on June 1 and lasts till November 30, with historically most occurring in September.

The north coast of the DR is conveniently situated between two fault lines, so small earthquakes are quite a common occurrence. Fortunately large earthquakes are fairly infrequent, the last one being in Puerto Plata and Santiago in 2003—at 6.2 on the Richter scale. The 2010 earthquake in Haiti was felt in most of the DR except the east, but of a far lesser intensity than the 7.0 magnitude experienced in Haiti.

THE PEOPLE

The Dominican Republic, in common with other Caribbean islands, has seen wave after wave of immigration, and present-day Dominicans are the result of several centuries of fusion of many different peoples and cultures. While much of the indigenous Taíno culture and societal organization ceased to exist a couple of generations after Spanish colonization, recent DNA studies have shown the persistence of indigenous ancestry in modern-day Dominicans. For the most part, ethnically Dominicans are a blend of African and European, as a result of the arrival of African slaves commencing in the sixteenth century combined with interregional migrations such as the African-Americans in Samaná and the Cocolos (English-speaking migrants from the British Caribbean islands) in the southeast.

The DR also has a significant number of people of Middle Eastern descent. These are mainly Christian Arabs from Syria, Lebanon, Jordan, and Palestine who started arriving in the late nineteenth century, many escaping persecution by Muslims, and another wave migrating in the wake of the escalation of conflict in the Middle East in the mid-twentieth century. Italian and Chinese immigrants started arriving in the country in the late nineteenth and throughout the twentieth century. After the Evian Conference of 1938, the dictator Trujillo was one of the few heads of state who offered to accept 200,000 Jewish refugees from Nazi persecution into the DR, although only a few hundred came. This was not as altruistic a move as it sounds: it was done partly to redeem Trujillo's international image after the 1937 Parsley Massacre (see A Brief History, below) and partly to "whiten" the population of the DR.

Migrants from Haiti could number as many as one million. Haiti is much poorer than the DR, and thousands of Haitians have migrated or been brought to the country over the years to work in agriculture, mainly sugarcane harvesting and construction, as well as many other low-income, low-status jobs. The Italians and Middle

Easterners, on the other hand, have flourished economically and politically, and their surnames are prominent among the rich and powerful sectors of Dominican society.

In the late twentieth century, North American, British, and European expatriates began moving to the DR, and more recently there has been an influx of Russian and other Eastern European arrivals.

A BRIEF HISTORY

The dates and facts of the Dominican Republic's history have less significance, perhaps, than the emerging themes, many of which have resonance today. Themes such as colonization, exploitation, slavery, foreign occupation, dictatorship, resistance, patriotism, and repeating the same mistakes fill the canvas on which is painted the DR of today and the psyche of its people. The Dominican Republic is the site of the first permanent European settlement in the Americas, although Columbus had visited the Bahamas and Cuba before landing on the island he named Hispaniola in December 1492.

But Dominican history did not start in 1492. Taíno Indians had settled the land five thousand years before Columbus's arrival; they are believed to have been a mix of two waves of migrants, one from Central America, probably from Yucatán or Belize, and the other from South America— Arawak Indians from Amazonia who passed through the Orinoco Valley in Venezuela and thence by canoe to the Caribbean islands.

Columbus's Journal, 1492
"Each of these islands had a great number of canoes, built of solid wood, narrow and not unlike our double-banked boats in length and shape, but swifter in their motion; they steer them only by the oar. These canoes are of various sizes, but the greater number are constructed with eighteen banks of oars, and with these they cross to the other islands, which are of countless number, to carry on traffic with the people. I saw some of these canoes that held as many as seventy-eight rowers."

The Taíno were peace loving and hospitable, which, together with the presence of gold, made them easy prey—as did the policy of appeasement of the invaders instituted by *cacique* (chieftain) Guacanagarix. The small settlement of Spanish sailors that Columbus left behind when he rushed

back to Spain with the good news exploited the indigenous population by forcibly taking their womenfolk as "servants," thereby, arguably, starting the sex industry in the DR. Taíno retaliation for this abuse was swiftly punished with the slaughter of the tribal chieftains; resistance thereafter took the form of escape to the mountains, from where the Taíno, led by *cacique* Enriquillo, launched sporadic attacks on the invaders. They were eventually wiped out by exposure to infectious diseases brought by the Europeans, enslavement, and social and cultural disintegration. After the Spanish had depleted the gold stocks, many settlers moved on to Mexico where silver had been discovered; on Hispaniola the colonists devoted themselves to agriculture and farming.

In 1665, French settlement on the west of the island was officially recognized by Louis XIV and the new French colony was named Saint-Domingue. In 1697, Spain formally ceded the western third of the island to France. The Spanish part became known as Santo Domingo. The next invaders were the buccaneers, pirates who attacked Spanish and French ports and shipping in the Caribbean in the late seventeenth century, and Hispaniola became part of the French and Spanish colonial turf wars.

French Rule

Both the Spanish and the French imported African slaves to work the sugarcane fields, and it was on the basis of their toil that Hispaniola prospered. Exploitation of the slaves was extremely cruel, and it is hardly surprising that a resistance movement, or slave revolt, arose in 1791, partially inspired by the French Revolution and led by Toussaint L'Ouverture. The slaves' struggle for freedom was intertwined with French aspirations to control all of Hispaniola and Spanish determination that they should not.

In 1795 Spain ceded Santo Domingo to France, and Napoleon sent a mission to quell the slave revolt; it failed disastrously and so, in 1804, independent Haiti was born in the west of the island. After France invaded Spain in 1808, the *criollos* (descendants of Spanish colonists) of Santo Domingo revolted against French rule and, helped by Great Britain and Haiti, reinstated Spanish sovereignty on the eastern side of the island. They then reintroduced slavery, to the alarm of the freed Haitians. Fearful that the French would launch another attack from Santo Domingo, in 1822 the Haitian President Jean-Pierre Boyer sent an army into eastern Hispaniola. The invasion succeeded; the Haitians once again abolished slavery there and incorporated Santo Domingo into the Republic of Haiti.

Haitian Rule and Independence
There followed twenty-two years of what Dominicans call the "Haitian Occupation," and it has been suggested that current anti-Haitian sentiment in the DR stems from the resentment

of that occupation felt by the former Spanish ruling class. Boyer nationalized all public and much private property and drafted young men into the (unpaid) Haitian army. He remodeled the economy but was opposed by Dominican farmers. The period of Haitian rule saw the emergence of an underground resistance group, La Trinitaria, under the leadership of Juan Pablo Duarte. Duarte, Ramón Matías Mella, and Francisco del Rosario Sánchez were decisive in the fight for independence, and they are now hailed as the founding fathers of the Dominican Republic. On February 27, 1844, the *Trinitarios* declared independence from Haiti.

Unfortunately, the maxim "Be careful what you ask for" applied, and having gained independence the Dominican Republic was then set on a course of internal struggle as it lurched from corrupt government to brutal dictatorship. In the following decades, there was a failed reunion with Spain (1861–65) and an American attempt at annexation. The dictatorship of General Ulises Heureaux came to a halt with his assassination in 1899, but not before he had plunged the country into a debt of fifteen times the annual budget. This was achieved mainly through heavy borrowing from American and European banks and the printing of US$5 million worth of unsecured paper money, known as the *papeletas de Lilís*, ruining many of the country's merchants.

Enter the United States

Once again, foreign powers entered the DR. Initially this was under an economic guise—President Theodore Roosevelt negotiated an agreement for the US to take on the DR's massive debt in exchange for customs receipts—but US investors in the sugar industry were worried by political instability and thus in 1916 President Woodrow Wilson ordered in the Marines. The US occupation of the DR lasted eight years but set in train a course of events that reverberated for the next fifty: the Americans left behind their love of baseball, which has surely enabled stellar sports careers for many Dominicans, and they also left a trained army, the head of which was a former telegraph clerk by the name of Rafael Leonidas Trujillo.

The Trujillo Dictatorship

In 1930 Trujillo took complete control, technically by means of an "election" where he gained 95 percent of the vote. He then established a

dictatorship that remained in power for more than thirty years using intimidation, torture, and assassination of political foes to terrify and oppress the population. Dominicans over the age of sixty will have lived through this period as children, and will certainly have internalized the tales their parents told them. It is perhaps not surprising that elderly Dominicans are loath to buck the system; any display of independence during the dictatorship tended to be a terminal activity. In 1937 the Parsley Massacre—so called because interrogators used the pronunciation of the word *perejil* (parsley) as a test to distinguish between darker-skinned Dominicans and Haitians—killed an estimated 17,000 to 35,000 Haitians living in the DR over a five-day period.

The killing of the Mirabal sisters (see page 63) in 1960 became the symbol of the covert but active Dominican resistance to Trujillo's regime. Trujillo was eventually murdered by members of his own armed forces (Antonio de la Maza, Salvador Estrella Sadhalá, Lieutenant Amado García Guerrero, General Antonio

Imbert Barrera, Pedro Livio Cedeño and others) on May 30, 1961, when he was seventy-one years old. According to an internal memorandum, the CIA Office of Inspector General's investigation into Trujillo's murder disclosed "quite extensive Agency involvement with the plotters."

Fifty years later, there is still much about this period that does not get spoken about openly in the DR. Clearly Trujillo could not have stayed in power as long as he did without the support of the US government, the Dominican elite, and the Roman Catholic Church. The US government saw him as a staunch supporter of their stand against the "evils of communism," but this ideological support wore a bit thin when he started fleecing US nationals economically by taking control of major American-owned industries in the DR, in particular the very important sugar industry. As for the role of the Dominican elite and the Roman Catholic Church, suffice it to say that this tends not to be discussed at upper-crust dinner parties.

Post-Dictatorship

Thereafter—as Dedé Mirabal, the surviving Mirabal sister, put it—Dominicans became free to choose their own bad leaders. When they chose potentially good ones, external influences interfered: the first democratically held elections returned Juan Bosch, whose leftist program was judged to be too extreme by a US administration paranoid about the possible spread of communism after Fidel Castro's successful revolution in Cuba. In 1963 President Bosch's government drafted a new, more liberal constitution that separated Church and state, put severe limits on the political activities of the armed forces, and established a wide range of civil liberties. Seven months later the Dominican Army, with the support of the CIA, engineered a coup d'état to oust Bosch from the presidency.

The following two years of chaos under military rule and resistance to it saw the nearest the DR has ever come to a full-scale revolution. An alliance of dissatisfied working-class groups and a dissident Army faction rose in rebellion and took action to reestablish constitutional order (as per the 1963 Constitution) on April 24, 1965. At this point, President Lyndon Johnson ordered an invasion by the US military on the pretext that the lives of American citizens in the DR needed to be protected. The real reason was the fear that the *Constitucionalistas* would bring about another Cuba. Elections in 1966, supervised by US forces and generally agreed to have been rigged, resulted in Joaquín Balaguer, right-hand man of Trujillo, gaining the presidency, which he subsequently hung on to for a long time.

Balaguer was responsible for an ambitious infrastructure program and for overseeing the DR's economic transition from a cash crop economy (sugar) to one dominated by tourism, industrial free zones, and remittances, as the mass emigration of Dominicans, mainly to the United States, gathered pace. Yet Balaguer also exemplified *caudillismo* (strongman tactics fused with clientelism), particularly evident in the repression of human rights and civil liberties, and the growing disparity between rich and poor continued to increase. The 1994 election was generally agreed to be fraudulent and was noted as such by international observers, but instead of stepping down, President Balaguer did a deal for a two-year (instead of four-year) term, with an election in 1996. This latter election was won by President Leonel Fernández of the Dominican Liberation Party (PLD).

While this period was an economically profitable one for the DR, resources were not plowed into social reform and the 2000 election was won by the opposition Dominican Revolutionary Party (PRD) under Hipólito Mejía. The PRD was supported, in the main, by the poor, who did not deserve the economic meltdown that was to follow with the collapse of Banco Intercontinental. Small wonder, then, that in 2004 President Fernández was elected to a second term of office with an absolute majority and the second-highest percentage ever in Dominican history (57 percent). In what looks suspiciously like an almost Balaguer-type yearning to hang on to the presidency, he was elected again in 2008— and changes to the Constitution ratified in 2010 now allow for future periods in office.

As they labor for poor wages in the free trade zones, in hotels, and in service to foreign expatriates, Dominicans sometimes ask themselves whether the "liberation" that the Mirabal sisters died for has achieved anything more than the positioning of their country as a vacation hotspot for *gringos*. Indeed, Dominican intellectuals are asking the same question: the 2008 United Nations Development Report on the Dominican Republic entitled "Human Development: A Matter of Power" pointed out that the current model for economic growth in the DR simultaneously creates wealth *and* generates poverty. Nowhere is this demonstrated more starkly than in the report's findings about the two main tourist provinces of Puerto Plata on the north coast and La Altagracia on the east coast (Punta Cana); in tourist areas, living conditions for Dominicans are below the national average.

GOVERNMENT

The DR is a representative democracy, with national powers divided among what are theoretically independent executive, legislative, and judicial branches. The president of the DR appoints the cabinet, executes laws passed by the Congress, and is commander in chief of the armed forces. The president and vice president are elected by direct vote for four-year terms. Legislative power is exercised by a bicameral Congress composed of the Senate and the Chamber of Deputies. Elections are held

every four years at the congressional level as well as every four years at the presidential level but not for the same four-year stretch, so in practice the political madness erupts every two years. In early 2010 the revisions to the Constitution were finally completed; one of the changes being implemented is the synchronization of presidential, congressional, and municipal elections, which will start in 2016.

THE ECONOMY

The DR's economy has traditionally depended on agriculture. Although sugarcane is the chief crop and sugar is an important export, production has declined sharply in recent years. Other major crops are coffee, cocoa, tobacco, and rice, as well as organic bananas, cacao, and coffee.

In the 1970s and 1980s the government began to diversify the economy and to place more emphasis on mining, tourism, and manufacturing. There are viable deposits of nickel, bauxite, gold, and other minerals. The establishment of free trade zones led to an increase in light industry, especially the manufacture of textiles and clothing, but recently competition from Asia has resulted in factory closures. Tourism and remittances from expatriate Dominicans are also important to the economy; both have been adversely affected by the global economic problems of 2009. Efforts at diversification have not lessened the gap between rich and poor or alleviated poverty in the DR.

WAYS OUT OF POVERTY

As we shall see, the DR is a highly stratified society with little upward social mobility and with social class determining access to power and position. Thus the children of the rich get the benefits of a private, bilingual education and top universities at home and abroad, followed by automatic entry into the family business or a profession with high earning potential, while everyone else does not. For the masses, job prospects include the free trade zone factories or the tourism industry, setting up or working in small entrepreneurial ventures like hair salons, working in *colmados* (corner grocery stores), street selling, purchasing a small motorbike and working as a messenger or a *motoconcho* (motorbike taxi) driver, unskilled menial work, domestic work, the sex industry, and migration.

The Dominican poverty trap is a result mainly of the country's education system, but also of a job market where connections are key. Those who do manage to complete high school (only about 10 percent in the state sector) can go on to study at the state university, UASD, where fees are modest but financial help with living costs is not available for the majority. For qualified young Dominicans from a poor background, lack of connections will be the main reason for lack of success, but employment in the retail sector, banking, or teaching will hoist them into the outer edge of the middle classes. Wages in these professional sectors are still very low, and it is common for people to supplement their incomes with other activities such as selling on commission.

"Instant" wealth is only available to those who fulfill every poor boy's dream and become a baseball player in the USA, or alternatively a musical star. Other formulas for success include marrying a rich *gringo*, becoming a drug dealer . . . or going into politics. It is no wonder that so many young people decide to emigrate. Only a very few do so legally; the rest resort to illegal methods such as risky *yola* (small boat) crossings to Puerto Rico. While many dream of a brighter future, only a few achieve it; the majority "know their place," even defining themselves as "*pobre*" (poor). The attitudes of other classes to the poor vary, but the foreign visitor should not be surprised at the greater tolerance of Dominicans toward begging. Restaurants in tourist areas will forbid entry by beggars because many tourists are offended by them, whereas patrons of Dominican restaurants, acknowledging their own good fortune, do not begrudge a few pesos to those in need. Food will also be given to the hungry at *colmados*.

THE MOVE FROM COUNTRYSIDE TO TOWN

The DR is a fascinating mix of old and new: gleaming, modern skyscraper buildings in parts of Santo Domingo and *barrios populares* (urban slums) in other parts, state-of-the-art medical facilities alongside *campo* (rural community) clinics bereft of supplies, the omnipresence of cell phones alongside the lack of electricity to power a radio. The population shift from countryside to town in search of employment has facilitated the development of *barrios*, some of which could be described as slums. Inevitably this has meant the decrease of extended family households, but not of extended family loyalty.

The turbulent history of the forging of the Dominican Republic gives clues as to what it is that makes Dominicans tick. They are, above all else, resilient. Their own governments over the years have thrown just about everything imaginable at them, yet they still do not lose their optimism, possibly because they are sustained by a deep-seated spirituality and an indomitable disposition.

chapter two

VALUES & ATTITUDES

THE ROLE OF THE FAMILY

The importance of the family in the Dominican Republic cannot be overstressed. In terms of loyalties, these lie with the family first and foremost, and this means the extended family. Virtually anyone with the same surname is a *primo*—literally "cousin," but also meaning a member of the same "tribe." In fact, Dominican society could described as a tribal or collectivist culture in which members are expected to help each other. This is clearly evident in the behavior

of expatriate Dominicans who remit money home to care not just for their immediate family but also for extended family members. An expatriate Dominican daughter may well have left her own children in the care of her mother, sisters, or aunts while she goes abroad to gain employment at a higher salary, much of which she then sends back each month to support her family.

The role of the mother in the family is accorded much respect, particularly by her sons, and the role of the grandmother even more so (the nature of the Dominican family is discussed in Chapter 4). Families in the DR care for their elderly, which is just as well, since state provision is lacking. As a foreign visitor you should thus not be surprised if the locals seem extremely interested in finding out about your family, particularly if you are traveling without them.

RELIGION

The extent to which belief in God permeates everyday life in the DR may come as a considerable cultural surprise for foreign visitors, especially in view of the Dominicans' hedonistic, live-for-the-moment approach to life. As well as a strong belief in God, there is also an omnipresent spirituality among the people, particularly among the old and poor. This outlook could be part of the reason for their joyous generosity toward others, but it is also convenient for those sectors of society determined to reinforce the powerlessness of the poor: you will put up with a lot in this life if you believe that your rewards will be forthcoming in the next!

Theory and Practice

Many Dominicans will not refer to a future event without saying "*Si Dios quiere*" ("God willing") and will not let a positive statement go by without thanking God for allowing it to happen ("*Gracias a Dios*"). A compliment, especially when directed to a baby or a small child, has to be accompanied by "*Dios lo/la bendiga*" ("God bless him/her"), without which a comment on the child's beauty, size, or good health is tantamount to tempting fate or invoking *mal de ojo*—the evil eye.

The constant reference to God in everyday conversation is not just idiomatic. Many Dominicans do genuinely believe in divine intervention, even for the most mundane of reasons. This conviction manages to coexist with decidedly less reverent social mores: the widespread acceptance of male infidelity, the traditional practice of having two or more parallel families, a rising underage pregnancy rate, early sexual initiation, open prostitution, and more. The way in which people reconcile their beliefs and practices is an expression of the competing tensions between the economic, the psychological, and the spiritual. To a certain extent, the objects of worship are viewed not so much as judgmental watchdogs or moral guides, but as talismans that protect against harm.

There is no doubt, however, that Dominicans view a lack of belief extremely negatively; atheists or agnostics are advised to be discreet and tactful if asked about religion Not being a Catholic or a Christian is one thing; not believing in God is a different matter.

PATRIOTISM, REGIONALISM, AND PAROCHIALISM

As in any collectivist culture where people tend to define themselves as members of groups (families, work units, tribes, nations) and usually consider the needs of the group to be more important than the needs of individuals, Dominicans' primary loyalty to family is followed by loyalty to close friends and the neighborhood group. With recent increased mobility in the DR and the move from rural to urban settings, this is evident in the immediate pleasure with which people greet even a stranger who comes from the same hamlet.

Despite recent massive migrations from country to town, there are many Dominicans who never stray beyond the outskirts of their particular village and for whom a journey to the capital has all the challenges of undertaking a pilgrimage; this parochialism can lead to the belief that all of the DR operates in the same way as the village. It also leads to fierce loyalty to one's particular turf. Dominicans are fiercely patriotic, molded by a history of invasion, occupation, and foreign exploitation, the last of which, some would argue, continues today.

CLASS IN SOCIETY

Dominican society is glaringly stratified. The Spanish colonizers introduced this system and the *caudillos* (the strongmen rulers of the country) maintained it; recent governments could be said to have reinforced it because they have done little to change it. This means that a handful of historically prominent families holds a great deal of the wealth and power. There is little social mobility, although the children of those working in recently developing occupations, such as tourism management, will have access to higher education abroad and thus the potential for some upward social mobility when they return.

Generally speaking, social class determines access to power and position, although the demarcation lines are less stark in the larger cities. Status, on the other hand, is defined more by family background than by absolute wealth. The newly developed narcotics industry has produced some very wealthy people, but all the outward trappings of wealth do not accord status or "couth."

CLIENTELISM

The historical role of the *caudillos*, with their self-aggrandizement through a system of clientelism, meshed easily with traditional Dominican values of the role of the family and the importance of interpersonal relationships. While the social system of relatively powerful and rich "patrons" promising to provide relatively powerless and poor "clients" with jobs, protection, infrastructure, and other benefits in exchange for votes and other forms of loyalty, including labor, might suggest a kind of "socioeconomic mutualism," these relationships are typically exploitative, often resulting in the perpetual indebtedness of the clients in what has been described as a "debt-peonage" relationship.

NEPOTISM

Nepotism, while prevalent, cannot thus have the same meaning in the DR as it does in societies where achievement is linked to merit, ability, or qualification. Since the family is the first reference point for loyalty, nepotism implies employing people one knows and trusts, which is of primary importance. Recent political scandals in the DR over nepotism in the Public Transport Office, the Blackouts Reduction Program, the State Electricity Corporation, and the National Hydraulic Resources Institute were met with official condemnation, but this tends to be lip service in a culture where many would also appoint their family members if they were in a position to do so.

POWER AS A RARE COMMODITY

Power is concentrated in the hands of the few; those who have it are determined to hang on to it, and those who have just a little will play it for all it is worth. Thus the obstacles invented by low-level bureaucrats might be set up in order to gain financial advantage, but can equally be to do with establishing the bureaucrat's place in the pecking order. Even in the family, older siblings can be seen ordering their younger brothers and sisters to carry out household tasks in ways that seem despotic to an outsider! This could be the result of a patriarchal model of the family and the macho conduct it engenders, although in the DR this tends to be class specific, or it could be the result of families internalizing autocratic models of government. Many lower-class families are in fact matriarchal due to absent fathers. The common expression "*Si Dios quiere*" ("God willing") expresses the belief that personal power is intertwined with one's place in the family, the community, and the grand design of God in ways a foreigner might deem tyrannical.

"Si Dios Quiere"
When our cleaning lady was leaving the house having finished her work, I would always thank her and remind her that I would see her on Thursday (or whatever day she was next due to appear)—and always this was met with "*Si Dios quiere.*" I learned to resist the temptation to say, "Not if God wishes, if *I* wish—I'm the one who pays the salary," because this would not have gone over well! (GB)

RACE
The stratification of Dominican society is also played out in its racial distribution: 16 percent of the population are white, 11 percent are black, and the vast majority, 73 percent, are mixed race or mulatto, according to most guidebooks. The meanings Dominicans put on those statistics may surprise visitors. The media researcher and writer Roland Soong has identified the plethora of names used to describe every conceivable shade of color and ethnic composition in Latin America, and the DR is no exception: the terms *morena* (brown), *india* (Indian), *blanca oscura* (dark white), and *trigueño* (wheat-colored) are bound

to be heard. As with other Latin American countries, the rich and powerful tend to be lighter skinned and the poor and powerless tend to be darker skinned. In contrast to people of African ancestry in other countries, however, Dominicans do not self-identify as black, even though, according to a leading Dominican scholar in the USA, Silvio Torres-Saillant, some 90 percent of the population have African ancestry.

Bewilderment

Outside observers, particularly African-Americans, can be somewhat bewildered that Dominicans have not used their blackness as a collective banner to advance their economic, cultural, or political cause. This leads to accusations that Dominicans are in denial over their African roots. It also leads to a lot of acrimony when the subject is discussed, so much so that some of my Dominican friends became quite upset with me when they heard I was writing about this! (GB)

The struggles for social justice and equality undertaken by people of color in the USA mean that blackness is their primary identity; when they encounter Dominican reluctance to identify in the same way, they can assume that this needs urgent corrective treatment. This attitude will go over no better in the DR than will colonialist, imperialist behavior by white visitors.

Into this mix should be added the Dominican Diaspora, those Dominicans who emigrated to the USA or were born there: Dominican poetess Sherezada Chiqui Vicioso is often quoted as saying, "Until I came to New York, I didn't know I was black." While Dominicans returning to live in the DR bring with them an awareness of the political construction of race as seen in the USA, not all are as eminent as Chiqui Vicioso. Many returning deportees, for example, might find their new political awareness is given less attention than their criminal past.

"Deracionalized Consciousness"
Instead of viewing Dominicans as being in denial over their African roots, it might be helpful to look at their self-image as an understanding of race that is not just biologically but also nationally and socially determined. Torres-Saillant refers to this as a "deracionalized consciousness," and it has both positive and negative outcomes: on the negative side, this attitude was manipulated by Trujillo in support of his negrophobic agenda in the Haitian massacre, the consequences of which are still with us today in the form of *antihaitianismo*. The positive outcome of deracionalized consciousness is that it is good for mental health and self-image. You can't, for example, accuse Dominicans of self-loathing! As Torres-Saillant says, "Their ability to step outside the sphere of their blackness has enabled them to remain whole."

In fact, for Dominicans to import another culture's construction of race (such as that of North America) would be a form of denial, inasmuch as they would be disregarding the complexity of their own experience of interracial relations. Ginetta E. B. Candelario's book *Black behind the Ears* argues that any serious effort to understand Dominican ideas and practices of race at home as well as in the Diaspora requires a large conceptual framework, informed by a cultural history of Dominican nation-building projects, the difficult plight of the Haitian Republic in the midst of a negrophobic world, the impact of US racial thought, and the Latin American glorification of the Hispanic heritage. In other words, there are more types of "reality" than just what is visible. There is also what is audible: one would be hard-pressed to deny African influence in Dominican music and dance. In fact, music and dance are a good example of the gap between the DR's dominant Hispanocentric ideology and its cultural reality.

At the end of the day, what matters is not how the reader, the writer, or a foreign black consciousness movement defines race, but how Dominicans define it.

Antihaitianismo

According to the political scientist Ernesto Sagás, "*Antihaitianismo* is actually the present manifestation of the long-term evolution of racial prejudice, the selective interpretation of historical facts, and the creation of a nationalist Dominican false consciousness. That process, of course, did not take place spontaneously. It was orchestrated by powerful elite groups in the Dominican Republic with strong interests to defend." Colonial elites emphasized the Hispanic culture of the Santo Domingo colonists versus the French and, later, the Haitians. According to them, the colonists of Santo Domingo were white, Catholic, and had a Hispanic culture. The Haitians, in particular, represented the opposite and the worst; they were black voodoo practitioners who had an African culture with a thin French veneer. Under the Haitian occupation the colonial elites found themselves at the mercy of Haitian army officers, many of whom were ex-slaves themselves, with little or no education, and who lacked the finesse and manners that the elites regarded so highly. Many of the elite families left the DR; Balaguer's perception of this was that "we lost some of our best families."

Such feeling might have been understandable at a time of Haitian "occupation," but it persisted long after Haiti had given up its aspirations to rule the entire island. In this context it is useful to see its perpetuation as a tool of national cohesion and domination, used by the Dominican elites to reinforce their position. Late nineteenth- and early twentieth-century literature and poetry exalted "Dominican" traits, while denigrating Haitian influences to the point of making them appear barbaric. At the same time the cult of the Taíno hero Enriquillo gave rise to the *indigenista* literary movement after the publication of the novel *Enriquillo* by Manuel de Jesús Galván in 1909.

Trujillo, apart from authorizing the Parsley Massacre in 1937, also used intellectuals like Balaguer to rewrite the history of Haitian–Dominican relations. Balaguer's book *La Realidad Dominicana* (1947) was considered the most brilliant defense of the Trujillo regime and "proved" that Haitians and Dominicans belong not only to different nations, but also to completely different races. This argument became part of the official credo, and although *antihaitianismo* is no longer part of the state's official ideology, unsurprisingly, it has stuck. Dominican children in school learn a national history full of distortions, myths, and prejudices, and reproduce it to their children. Thus it is that when a Haitian in the DR commits a homicide he is likely to experience swift "justice" at the hands of a lynch mob who feel justified in taking such action. There are a number of NGOs working to foster collaborative efforts between Haitians and Dominicans, and the Dominican reaction of mobilizing assistance for Haiti after the catastrophic earthquake of January 2010 is but one indication that when the chips are really down, Haitians can be perceived as "brothers in need."

THE *MAÑANA* SYNDROME

Most visitors will have some understanding that Latino notions of punctuality are different from those found in colder climates, but they might not know why. We have already seen that relationships are very important to Dominicans—far more important than schedules and being on time for appointments. If Dominicans run into an old friend, even on the way to an important meeting, they will probably choose to chat and will find it very difficult to interrupt the conversation; they will most likely prefer to be late for the meeting, favoring relationships over punctuality. In the DR it is worth checking, with a smile, whether the time given for an appointment is "Dominican time" or US/European time.

Dominican Time

My husband was running late for his second meeting of the morning because participants at his first meeting were late, so at 11:00 a.m. he telephoned ahead, to be told "We close at 8:00 p.m." "Gracious, I won't be *that* late. I should be there at 2:30 p.m. [instead of 2:00 p.m.]." "Oh, OK. So why are you calling?" Anything up to 90 minutes late is not considered late in the DR. (GB)

Mañana, it should be noted, does not necessarily mean tomorrow. What it does mean is "not today." It could mean tomorrow, or the day after, or the week after, or even sometime never. If it means the latter, additional nonverbal clues may be given. People in collectivist cultures have a hard time saying "no"—it is almost considered a rude word—so they will say "yes," but with the sort of reluctance that shows that they mean "no."

DOMINICAN OPTIMISM

"Yes" with reluctance, meaning "no," can sometimes be misconstrued as lying. A common moan of new expatriates in the DR is that Dominicans tell lies. Such stereotyping is no truer of Dominicans than of any other nationality. What it fails to take into account is Dominican optimism—I want it to be so, ergo it is so. Dominicans do not want to tell you things you do not want to hear, because this could negatively impact on the interpersonal relationship. The only way to overcome this is to make sure you are giving no signals about what it is you want to hear: the question "It isn't far to the center of town, is it?" will always elicit the response "No, it isn't far," even if it is three bus journeys and two hours away. Better to take the time to ask how far, how long, how many bus journeys—be sure to ask one question at a time, however, or it will only be the last one that gets answered.

Just as people have a hard time saying "no," they also have a hard time saying "I don't know." Instead, they will tell you what they want to be true: yes, you can get a direct bus to Higuey today; yes, you can climb to the top of Pico Duarte in a couple of hours. One needs to make informed judgments about who is most likely to know, and ask them. There is no need to burst the bubble of Dominican optimism (as if you could!) by becoming confrontational on receiving inaccurate information—after all, if you take optimism away from powerless people, what do they have left?

REACTIVE, NOT PROACTIVE

Volunteering information is not the norm, either; this can also be frustrating for the visitor. The Dominican reluctance to volunteer information is particularly acute among government bureaucrats, and to a foreigner it can feel as if one is being singled out and given the runaround. It happens to Dominicans too, however, and many do not challenge it. The older population, with their memories of the dictatorship, are the least likely to want to make waves and almost display what could be called "learned helplessness." Without that compliance they would not have achieved their advanced years, so it was certainly a useful skill.

Ask the Right Question!
Three times I went to collect a check that my partner was owed; each time, there was no check. When I subsequently asked for his *money*, I was given cash right away. My fault for having asked the wrong question! (GB)

ATTITUDES TO FOREIGNERS

Dominican warmth, friendliness, helpfulness, and hospitality are legendary. They are very curious about others and forthright in asking questions. When a Dominican asks "How are you?" they really want to know. This is at sharp variance with those cultures where any answer beyond "Fine, thanks" is seen as an imposition. Dominicans have *time* for you. They expect to learn all about you and pass it on to others: the common expression "There are no secrets in Puerto Plata" is true. What can be disconcerting for the foreigner is when they pass it on to others *in front of you*—the next person to join the group gets told your story by the person you told it to. There's no need to take offense; this is quite normal in the DR.

Foreigners might be surprised at how deep and how fast Dominicans go into emotional and private topics in social conversations. The five culture communication levels, as identified by sociologist David Pollock and intercultural specialist Ruth Van Reken, go from "superficial" to "still safe," "judgmental," "emotional," and finally, to total "disclosure." Foreigners seem to need much more time in the superficial stage to develop trust and feel comfortable before going into private topics; for Dominicans, going too slowly would demonstrate a lack of interest and might even be a sign of coldness.

INTIMACY IS NOT TRUST

Readiness to share intimate details should not be mistaken for trust, however. When a Dominican tells someone their life history there is no expectation that it will be kept private, so such sharing does not denote trust. Trust is highly valued and not quickly or easily gained by outsiders, perhaps as a result of the human rights and economic abuses the people have suffered at the hands of the powerful. Dominicans are accustomed to foreigners arriving and departing, which is the norm for a tourism destination. Real trust will only be earned by staying and proving one's worth. Anyone whose car breaks down in the middle of the countryside will find several willing helpers almost immediately, however— they will probably disagree with each other vociferously as to the cause of the automotive problem, but they will help and should be rewarded, even if they refuse to take your gift in gratitude. It is OK to insist that they take it.

THE COAST IS NOT THE COUNTRY

There are marked differences in attitudes toward foreigners between tourist locations and other parts of the DR. Tourist locations in the DR, as elsewhere in the world, will attract less reputable Dominicans well versed in both the English language and an array of street scams, as well as prostitutes and, more recently, narcovendors (see Chapter 7). In tourist towns, foreigners get a lot of attention; inland they might be stared at, but a smile will break the ice. Away from tourist areas foreigners are not singled out for any special attention, so the experience is much more "normal."

REACTIONS TO CRITICISM

Dominicans from all walks of life do not react well to criticism by foreigners, whether it is a government minister criticized by the US ambassador or a shop assistant who is keen to deny responsibility for accidentally mischarging a foreign tourist. Many Dominicans have perfected the art of self-justification. It is not so much that they are prickly and defensive, because criticism from fellow Dominicans *is* accepted. It stems more from their historical experience: foreign powers have in the past pontificated without consultation with Dominicans, and at certain times, such as during the dictatorship, it was safer not to accept blame. There are acceptable ways in which the foreigner can handle this: being firmly and quietly self-confident, using humor, and being nonconfrontational are more likely to result in a satisfactory outcome. Losing one's cool is not!

"Progress" and globalization have hit the Dominican Republic in recent years, so in many ways this is a society in a state of flux. The clergy and ordinary Dominicans bemoan the demise of family values, although if you set the DR alongside the developed world, family values are much stronger here. In some respects it is a case of *plus ça change* in the DR: visit parts of the *campo* and you would think you had gone back a century. Indeed, this is part of what makes the land and its people so attractive.

chapter three

RELIGION, CUSTOMS, & TRADITIONS

RELIGION
Catholicism
The country's official religion is Catholicism (close to 90 percent of the population, although that

percentage is changing with the growth of Evangelical Protestant religions), and while churchgoing is not a universal pursuit, very few Dominicans would admit to not being religious on some level.

At the same time, relatively few Dominicans are baptized or confirmed, and not that many are married in the eyes of the Church. For reasons more economic and social than religious, the wealthy tend to be more active in their church attendance than most other sectors of the population, and at the other end of the spectrum, so are the poorest.

Evangelical Protestantism
Evangelical Protestant churches, meanwhile, are growing in popularity, appealing to converts from Catholicism. It is likely that these worshippers are

attracted to the emphasis on abstinence, moderation, and modesty, possibly as a reaction against the alarmingly high rate of domestic abuse, not to mention marital infidelity and deadbeat dads.

Earlier Protestants in the DR include the African-American liberated slaves who settled in the northeastern Samaná peninsula in the early nineteenth century, and the Cocolos from the English-speaking Caribbean islands who migrated to the southeast of the country in the later part of that same century to work in the growing sugar industry. Other minority Christian sects include the Jehovah's Witnesses, Seventh-Day Adventists, and Mormons.

Other Religions

Non-Christian beliefs do not register very strongly on the average Dominican's radar. If a person is not a Catholic, it is assumed that they are *evangélico*—that is, a Protestant. Nonetheless, Muslim, Jewish, and Buddhist communities are present on a very small scale, with their respective places of worship in Santo Domingo. In the case of the Jewish community, as well as the synagogue and community center in the capital, there is a synagogue in the north-coast town of Sosúa, site of the other main Jewish community.

THE CHURCH AND POLITICS

As in many other Catholic countries, in the Dominican Republic the Church has been active in politics, for better and for worse. The Catholic hierarchy was for a long time supportive of—even allied with—the Trujillo dictatorship.

God and Trujillo

Rafael Leonidas Trujillo's monumental ego meant that as well as having the capital city and the highest mountain in the country renamed in his honor, he also expected to be revered alongside God. This was expressed in the motto that had to be displayed in the entrance hall of every Dominican home between 1930 and 1961—"*Dios y Trujillo*"—alongside a portrait of the dictator and a religious painting. In return, Trujillo signed a Concordat with the Vatican in 1954 that bestowed special privileges on the Church in the Dominican Republic, overruling the more secular Constitution drawn up earlier in the century that separated Church and state.

There was a limit to the Church's tolerance of the excesses of the dictatorship, however. In 1960, the religious hierarchy ended up challenging Trujillo's repression in a boldly outspoken Pastoral Letter that was read from the nation's pulpits on Good Friday, which many believe was a crucial turning point in Dominican history. The letter helped break Trujillo's grip on the Dominican people and paved the way for his demise on May 30, 1961. Nonetheless, Trujillo's Concordat remains in effect today.

Minority religions led by the Evangelical alliance have tried to change what they see as the Catholic Church's privileged status on the grounds of discrimination, as the state funds Catholic institutions such as churches and schools. The Dominican Supreme Court has ruled against these bids on the grounds that the Constitution also guarantees freedom of worship to members of all religions.

It can't be denied that the Catholic Church still plays a prominent role in everyday affairs. The current Cardinal, Monsignor Nicólas de Jesus López Rodríguez, is not one to mince his words and is frequently heard denouncing everything from high-level government corruption to "homosexual bordellos" in his neighborhood, the Colonial Zone of Santo Domingo.

Liberation Theology

The more liberal elements of the Catholic Church, such as the Jesuits, who emphasize social justice and providing a voice for the poor and marginalized, are also active in the DR, working in the *bateyes* (sugar-cane settlements), *barrios populares* (urban slums), and poor *campos* (rural communities). Some of the more outspoken priests, such as Padre Rogelio Cruz, often appear to be a thorn in the side of the dominant conservative Church hierarchy as a result of their challenges to the status quo. There are also academic think tanks like Centro Juan Montalvo and NGOs like Jesuit Refugee Services.

POPULAR RELIGION

Popular religious expression combines Catholicism with elements of African worship, similar to *Santería* in Cuba and *Candomblé* in Brazil, where African deities are lightly camouflaged with the identity of Catholic saints. This dates back to the early days of the evangelization of the African slaves. Obliged to practice Catholicism by their Spanish masters and priests, they did so on the surface while maintaining their traditional beliefs beneath a layer of Christian symbolism.

The Gods and their Corresponding Saints

Similar to *Santería* in Cuba and *Candomblé* in Brazil, *religiosidad popular* in the Dominican Republic is the folk belief system that enabled African slaves to conceal their beliefs. Catholic saints stand in for traditional Yoruba deities known as *Orishas*, including Eleggua, the keeper of the roads and the world, associated with Saint Anthony. Obatala is known as the parent of the *Orishas* and all humankind and is associated with Our Lady of Mercy. Yemaya is the spirit of motherhood and is associated with the Virgin of Regla and Mary (Star of the Sea). Babalu Aye is the *Orisha* name for St. Lazarus. Chango, the god of thunder, probably one of the best-known *Orishas*, is honored on December 4, St. Barbara's Day.

Dominicans are divided on the question of whether these influences came directly from Africa, or whether they are a more recent "infiltration" by immigrants from neighboring Haiti: the debate is heavily political and is to do with a desire on the part of many Dominicans to distance themselves from their African origins, while others are eager to embrace them. Meanwhile, the Catholic Church in the DR is vocal in its hostility to anything that departs from orthodox tradition, labeling it as "pagan" or even "satanic."

Witch Doctors

A lot of Dominicans—urban as well as rural, rich as well as poor—while nominally Catholic, will still consult traditional *brujos* (witch doctors) and seek herbal remedies and magical amulets for physical and emotional ailments from *botánicas* (mystical herbalist shops). There is a certain degree of taboo surrounding this, and many people will not admit to it, but it is said to be popular across the social spectrum. *Brujos* may invoke evil spirits, but *curanderos* will seek to heal only, mainly in rural communities and among those unable to afford the services of a medical doctor.

GAGÁ

The word *gagá* describes a musical style, a ritual celebration, and the troupe of musicians and dancers taking part. The word is derived from— or related to—the Kreyol (Haitian Creole) word *rara*. There is no consensus on whether *rara* and *gagá* share common African origins, both coming

from Africa with the slaves who were brought to work in what is now Haiti and the DR, or whether *gagá* is just the Dominican version of *rara*, brought over by Haitian migrants. Although a *gagá* troupe can take part in a carnival, a *gagá* celebration is an event in itself.

Traditional groups like the Guloyas (the name either comes from the "David and Goliath" mime that they perform, or because these immigrants were referred to as "good lawyers") of San Pedro de Macorís, whose dance and mime performances were brought over by immigrants from St. Kitts in the English-speaking Caribbean, and Los Congos de Villa Mella have been declared UNESCO Masterpieces of the Oral and Intangible Heritage of Humanity. Los Congos—full name The Brotherhood of the Holy Spirit of the Congos of Villa Mella—is a three-hundred-year-old tradition of worshipping both the Holy Spirit of Christian tradition and the West African god of the dead, Kalunga.

Gagá

Some *gagá* celebrations are open to the public and easy to get to, like the annual *gagá* in Yamasá, which is held in late June to celebrate St. Anthony's Day (*el Día de San Antonio*). Yamasá is a short drive from the capital, and the event is held on the grounds of the Hermanos Guillén crafts center. A wide variety of spectators and participants come together from the big cities and towns as well as from surrounding rural areas to watch people engaging in traditional worship, which includes chanting, drumming, and praying. The arrival of the *gagá* is the climax of the occasion, when a large group of dancers and musicians beating drums and cracking whips invades the area in a thrilling, colorful, and noisy spectacle.

In the last decade, a group of urban-based Dominican rock musicians have promoted *gagá* and other traditional musical forms with fusion-style recordings. This has increased the popularity of these musical styles beyond the rural areas and brought them to a more middle-class, urban audience. Events like the San Antonio *gagá* are becoming so popular with people from the capital that they have begun to resemble pop festivals. Everyone is welcome.

These fascinating religious/folkloric celebrations are held in Baní, Guerra, Monte Plata, and many other parts of the country. Other forms of popular expression are *palos* (ritualized drumming) and *salves* (religious chanting).

RURAL CUSTOMS

Convite

The tradition of *convite*, shared with neighboring Haiti, is a wonderful example of community solidarity where members of rural communities come together for a specific task to benefit the community as a whole or a needy family.

Décimas

Décimas are ten-line poems that are popular in many parts of the Spanish-speaking world. In some rural areas, a visitor to the community will be received in a semiformal setting, and may not notice the person on the sidelines scribbling notes while the conversation takes place. At the close of proceedings, this person will prove to be more than just some routine minute taker when he or she stands up and recites a poem describing the events of the day and name checking the guests or visitors.

SUPERSTITIONS

More mundane beliefs and superstitions that may intrigue non-Dominicans are the common conviction that opening the fridge after ironing can cause permanent damage in the shape of a *pasmo* or spasm, or that the cool, humid night air (*el sereno*) has life-threatening properties. Newborn babies are given a jet or *azabache* bracelet to ward off the evil eye. Characters in Dominican folklore include the *ciguapa*, a woman whose feet point backward and who is said to roam the countryside at night luring unsuspecting victims, and the *cuco*, a bogeyman who is invoked by Dominican parents to make their children behave. Some of these beliefs are widely held, although usually (but not always) in inverse proportion to the believer's level of education.

NATIONAL HEROES

Several historical indigenous figures are part of the national pantheon, including *caciques* such as Hatuey and the Taíno princess Anacaona. The Taíno *cacique* Enriquillo had been baptized and educated by Catholic priests before leading the revolt against the Spaniards from the mountain range of Bahoruco.

Los Tres Padres de la Patria (the Three Founding Fathers)— Juan Pablo Duarte, Francisco del Rosario Sánchez, and Ramón Matías Mella—are held up as moral role models for Dominicans, the incarnation of patriotic values.

Las Hermanas Mirabal (the Mirabal sisters)—Patria, Minerva, and María Teresa— were active in the anti-Trujillo underground movement of the 1950s, leading to their murders on November 25, 1960, by the dictator's henchmen.

Colonel Francisco Alberto Caamaño Deñó was the leader of the *Constitucionalistas*, the army faction that rebelled against the junta that ousted President Juan Bosch in 1963. The April 1965 US invasion quelled this uprising; in 1973 the exiled Caamaño commanded a guerrilla invasion against the Balaguer regime, but was captured and executed.

Mamá Tingó (Florinda Soriano Muñoz) was a *campesina* (farmer) leader who was killed in a land-related dispute in 1974. Her iconic image— that of a black woman wearing a turban—has been adopted by rural women's groups as a symbol of their struggle for rights.

Orlando Martínez was a left-wing academic and journalist murdered by the authorities in 1975 after publishing an article critical of the government. His killing is considered one of the most notorious crimes of the "twelve years of Balaguer" (1966–78), a time when many Dominicans were imprisoned or killed for political reasons. The late president, who died in 2002, famously left a "blank page" in his autobiography, promising that after his death the true circumstances of Martinez's death would be revealed, but this has yet to happen.

RELIGIOUS CELEBRATIONS

The main dates in the Dominican calendar will be familiar to most Westerners, but the customs and celebrations associated with them do vary. Christmas (*Navidad*) and Easter (*Semana Santa*) are celebrated, Lent is observed, and although Carnival should precede Lent, celebrations always last throughout the month of February no matter when Mardi Gras falls in a particular year—much to the chagrin of the Church hierarchy.

Christmas and *Reyes*

At Christmastime the most important date is December 24—Christmas Eve or *Noche Buena*—when the family gets together and has a meal, traditionally of roast pork, rice with pigeon peas, Russian salad, spaghetti, and many other festive trimmings like *kipes* (*kibbes*, Middle Eastern-style wheat and meat patties), *pastelitos* (*empanadas* or pasties), a baguette-like bread known as *telera*, *ponche* (egg nog), and *sidra* (sparkling apple wine).

December 25, although a public holiday, is not such a special occasion—except in the north of the country, when it is the date for children to receive their Christmas gifts, not from Santa Claus but from *El Niño Jesús* (the Baby Jesus). Most Dominican children follow the Spanish tradition and do not receive their presents until January 6, or *el Día de los Tres Reyes Magos* (Three Kings Day, also known simply as *Reyes*), in whose honor a boisterous procession is held through Santo Domingo's Colonial Zone on the night of January 5. Although these traditions still endure, they are merging with the US-style imagery of Santa Claus, reindeer, and wintry scenes.

Gift giving is very much part of Christmas, and while Dominicans do spend a lot of money at this time of year (fueled by the "thirteenth check"—a bonus salary paid to most Dominican state and private sector employees in mid-December), gifts are mainly for children and not for every single family member, although practice varies from family to family. Christmas is a time when employers give their employees gifts, and business associates exchange tokens, usually food baskets or bottles of wine or spirits. Most families will help poorer relatives or acquaintances with a contribution to the Christmas Eve meal, in the shape of a gift basket or money. The exchanging of Christmas cards is not a common practice.

Easter, or *Semana Santa*

The most important date at Easter time is Good Friday, which is celebrated in traditional religious services and processions, but for most Dominicans Easter is not so much a time for religious reflection as it is an opportunity to take to the roads and hit the beaches and rivers, and eat the strange concoction of *habichuelas con dulce*—sweet creamed beans made with spices, sugar, condensed milk, and sweet potato.

Popular Fiestas

Fiestas patronales, or saints' days, are celebrated in rural areas. Each town has its patron saint, and the festivities held on the appropriate date can last for several days. These celebrations usually combine contemporary and traditional culture as expressed in church processions, popular rituals, live music, and all-night parties and sports tournaments.

Moveable Feasts

Sometimes when a holiday falls in the middle of the week, it is "moved" to the following Monday to create a long weekend. If it falls on a Tuesday or a Thursday and isn't moved, people will often take the Monday or Friday in between off as a holiday for an extra-long weekend, known as a "*puente*" (bridge). This rule usually—but not always—applies to nonreligious occasions.

CARNIVAL AND OTHER CELEBRATIONS

Carnival in the Dominican Republic is still spontaneous and rooted in tradition, despite some commercialization in recent years. While undeniably Dominican in flavor, Carnival in the DR shares many features with carnivals held around the Spanish-speaking world. Each city has

its own particular tradition of Carnival with its own typical characters or costumes. The Carnival of La Vega, a provincial town in the Cibao, is generally held to be the best and is

undeniably spectacular, but its very fame has meant that the city becomes engulfed with crowds, diminishing the authenticity of the event and attracting thieves and pickpockets. In more remote areas like Montecristi in the northwest, Cotui in the eastern Cibao, and Cabral in the southwest, Carnival has retained its traditional style.

Depending on where you are, *diablos cojuelos, mácaros, cachuas, toros,* or *papeluses* are different names for the characteristic horned devils in elaborate sharp-toothed masks and multicolored flamboyant costumes. Robalagallina is a traditional Carnival character portrayed by a garish female impersonator; others include the *Tiznaos,* who

blacken their skin with engine oil to depict Africans, and *Indios,* people dressed as Indians. Carnival is generally a once-yearly chance for men of all inclinations to indulge in a spot of socially sanctioned cross-dressing. Some troupes will simply enact a topical situation to delight the crowds, like imitating the president or some other public figure, complete with an entourage of mafia-style bodyguards. Something to watch out for at Carnival time is the practice of whacking fellow participants' and spectators' backsides with pig bladders, which can be quite painful.

Carnival processions are held throughout February. The grand finale takes place at the end of the month or at the beginning of March in Santo Domingo, where the winning *comparsas* (troupes) from each city come together for a procession along the city's Malecón seafront boulevard, coinciding with the February 27 Independence Day celebrations.

Other national celebrations of a nonreligious nature are dotted throughout the year. These are usually marked by a ceremony of some sort, but are not culturally significant. The flag is raised and the national anthem (known simply as *El Himno Nacional*) is played on these occasions, and also every morning at school assembly. The convention is to stand to attention with right hand over heart, or at least to stand quietly and respectfully.

OFFICIAL PUBLIC HOLIDAYS IN THE DOMINICAN REPUBLIC

New Year's Day January 1

Día de los Tres Reyes Magos (Three Kings Day) January 6

Altagracia Day (honoring of Our Lady of High Grace, protector of the DR) January 21

Duarte Day (honoring Juan Pablo Duarte, founding father of the DR) January 26

Independence Day February 27

Good Friday varies

Workers' Day May 1

Corpus Christi June 11

Restoration Day August 16

Las Mercedes (honoring Our Lady of Mercy, patron of the DR) September 24

Constitution Day November 6

Christmas Day December 25

FAMILY CELEBRATIONS
Baby Showers
One of several foreign traditions that have been embraced by Dominicans involves friends and relatives of a pregnant woman throwing a party in her honor, and "showering" her with gifts for the baby. The event is called by its English name—baby shower.

Baptism
As mentioned above, not all Dominicans are baptized even though they consider themselves Catholics. On the occasion of a baptism the godparents are expected to cover the cost of the celebration. When the baby grows up, he or she will often refer to the godparents as *madrina/padrino*. In turn, the *madrina/padrino* will refer to the baptized child as *ahijado/a*.

First Birthday
The first birthday party (*el primer año*) is an important event, possibly due to the fact that high infant mortality is still a recent memory and in some cases a reality for many Dominicans. The party is a celebration of the child's surviving the first year of life.

"Celebro tu Cumpleaños"
The singing of "Happy Birthday"—often in English, along with the Spanish version *"Cumpleaños Felíz"* and the Dominican *"Celebro tu Cumpleaños"*—and the cutting of the cake marks the end of the party and is a cue for guests to leave.

First Communion

Many Dominican families will celebrate their child's first communion (*primera comunión*) with a small party for friends and relations after the church service.

Quinceañera

When a girl turns fifteen, her parents will organize a *quinceañera* party, something between a "sweet sixteen" and a debutante's coming-out party. The rituals of the event—the change from flat shoes to high heels, the ball gown, the hairdo, and the first dance of the party with Dad—are supposed to  symbolize the girl's transition to womanhood. There is no formal equivalent for boys.

Birthdays

In general, birthdays (*fiesta de cumpleaños*) are celebrated with great attention to detail: the decorations are store-bought, cakes are not homemade but ordered, and the spread is lavish. This of course will vary according to class and purchasing power, but even poorer households spend freely for the occasion. Parents should note that they are expected to attend together with their children and socialize with the other adults. Beer and buffet food (*picadera*) are often laid out for the adult guests, while the children gorge themselves on the usual birthday fare.

Weddings

Perhaps surprisingly for such a religious culture, not everyone goes to the trouble of a religious wedding ceremony, and among the poorer social sectors couples don't even have a civil wedding. They tend instead to cohabit: their relationship is formalized when they move in together, and from then on they may refer to their spouse as *mujer* (wife) or *marido* (husband) (as opposed to *esposo* or *esposa*, which are usually used for formally married couples, although the distinction is not rigid).

Among the middle classes, a civil marriage ceremony followed by a small party at home for family and close friends is common. Only upper-middle-class and upper-class marriages will, in most cases, involve the full-blown church ceremony followed by a lavish reception.

Funerals

After a person dies, they are taken to a funeral parlor (*funeraria*) for an overnight wake (*velorio*), and it is there that friends, colleagues, and more distant relatives can pay their respects to the immediate family. The burial usually takes place the next day. As these things tend to happen fast, not everyone can make it to the wake or the funeral despite the social obligation requiring them to attend, so an additional way to express condolences is to go to the mass celebrated on the ninth day after the death, which marks the close of the nine-day deep mourning period. White and purple as well as black are the colors of mourning, and unlike in the Mediterranean, full black mourning dress is rarely seen in Dominican culture.

OTHER WIDELY OBSERVED OCCASIONS

Valentine's Day (*San Valentín, Día del Amor y la Amistad*, February 14) is not just for romantic lovers, but a general celebration of friendship. This includes between members of the same sex—if you are a female visitor with a Dominican woman friend, don't read it wrong if she gives you flowers on Valentine's Day!

International Women's Day (March 6) is a day where women and their contribution to society are celebrated, and all women will receive tokens and good wishes as a matter of course.

Secretary's Day (late April) is another significant date when offices empty at lunchtime as bosses take their admin staff out for a meal.

Mother's Day (last Sunday in May) is a huge deal: motherhood in general is feted, so mothers will be congratulated by all and sundry, not just their own children. Father's Day (last Sunday in July) is also celebrated, although with less fanfare.

Halloween (October 31) is increasing in importance although it does meet with some resistance from several quarters, some seeing it as a foreign imposition and others as a satanic ritual.

All Souls' Day (*El Día de los Muertos*, November 1) is when people visit the graves of loved ones.

None of these are public holidays, although Mother's Day always falls on a Sunday.

chapter four

DOMINICANS AT HOME

FAMILY LIFE

The classic nuclear, two-parent model is held up as the ideal family in the Dominican Republic, but the traditional extended structure is still alive and well, and female-headed households are on the increase. Some features of Dominican family life cross the social spectrum, while economics, demographics, and class determine other variations. Family ties are fundamental to Dominican life—the primary allegiance is to the immediate family, followed by the wider extended family and the local community.

Machismo, Matriarchy, and Polygamy
Machismo

In the Dominican Republic, as in most other traditional male-dominated societies, lack of education and options have meant that up till recently, women had little choice but to put up with parallel families, infidelity, and abuse. As Dominican women now outnumber men when it comes to university enrollment, this is set to change. Financial independence means that women are less likely to be trapped in an unhappy marriage. Correspondingly, the divorce rate is very high in the DR, which suggests that men have been slow to adjust to less submissive, more independent women.

Attitudes are also slowly changing in terms of the way children are socialized. Traditionally boys were not taught any domestic chores, while girls were expected to take part in household duties. Marriage at a young age meant that a girl would go directly from being a daughter to being a wife, and a boy would leave the care of his mother to be looked after by a wife, so there was no need for any independent skills. Now people generally get married later, and some spend a few years in between living independently. Many Dominicans still remain in the parental home until marriage, while studying at university, and/or working, however. The country's underlying machismo is still very much in evidence, but its absolute dominance is not as strong as it used to be.

Ritualized Matriarchy?
Female-headed households are common in the Dominican Republic for a number of reasons, including divorce, desertion, single parenthood, and emigration. Some estimates put the percentage of female-headed, one-parent homes in the Caribbean region at about 35 percent (the highest rate in the world), and the Dominican Republic is no exception. According to the ENHOGAR national public opinion survey conducted in 2005, 32 percent of Dominican households fall into this category. This is the case

across the social spectrum, although early sexual initiation and underage pregnancies are more common among the poorer classes due to lack of education and opportunities combined with lack of access to contraception.

In a traditional Dominican family, the mother is revered to the point that in many cases Mother's Day is given more importance than birthdays, yet a mother's status is more akin to that of a figurehead. Ultimately, power is almost always held by the males of the family—in the absence of a father, elder sons will take over that role.

Polygamy
Most Dominicans will have direct or indirect experience of de facto polygamy within their own families. More than just infidelity, this can manifest itself as a man having children with two or more women at the same time, sometimes openly, and in other cases covertly. In the rural areas especially, people describe situations where the man in question cohabited with two sisters, or set up home for his other woman and her children right next door to his main marital home. Although setups of this kind still exist, they are becoming less common—especially among urban middle-class families.

This is not to say that monogamy and fidelity are making a comeback. Many men still have affairs or mistresses, but factors like education, contraception, and professional and financial independence mean that a mistress is less likely to have children with him, and that his official wife is less likely to tolerate this behavior and may exercise the option of divorce. Still, it is not unheard of for previously unknown siblings to appear at even the most respectable man's funeral. These days, relationships are more likely to follow the serial monogamy mode.

Domestic Violence

Violence within the family is a major problem in the Dominican Republic, but in the last few years much has been done to increase awareness of the issue and to fight it. The statistics are still grim: the UN agency INSTRAW calculates that approximately two hundred women are killed by their partners each year. According to women's groups, the rate is six times higher than in Spain.

The causes are complex—it would be incomplete to attribute the high rate of domestic violence entirely to poverty and machismo, especially as the problem is not confined to the poorer sectors. As in many other cultures, however, the belief still lingers that a man has the right to beat his wife, and there is a generalized attitude that whatever happens between a couple is their private business. Legislation and public awareness campaigns are addressing this, but it is not a change that is likely to happen overnight.

Children, Fertility, and *Jamonas*

The birthrate has fallen dramatically over the last couple of generations, as a result of improved education and increased levels of affluence. The fall is most evident among the urban middle class,

but even in the rural areas where it was common to find families with over ten, even twenty children, this has been reduced considerably.

Poor people viewed their children as future providers, and the need to have a large family was traditionally partly related to the fact that many children were expected to die in infancy. Children from poorer households are, however, still expected to support their parents, while the children of wealthier parents are given many things that would be considered luxuries even in more affluent countries. The other factor in the declining birthrate is the increasing knowledge, availability, and acceptance of birth control over the last thirty years.

The average number of children born to the average Dominican woman stands at about three—a couple of generations back, it was closer to six. Women tend to marry and/or have children early. Again, this is more the case in poorer social sectors where underage motherhood is still a common phenomenon. Although this is changing, it is still uncommon for a Dominican woman to wait beyond her late twenties before having her first child, even in professional, educated, and affluent circles. A woman who has not married by her late twenties is still labeled a *jamona*—an old maid.

The Elderly

As a rule, elderly people are at the center of family life. In their later years they are cared for in the family home as opposed to being sent to retirement homes, and this is one element commonly cited as proof that Dominicans (together with other Latin cultures) are more family oriented than their Anglo-Saxon cousins. It also helps that the availability of cheap labor means it is affordable to hire round-the-clock caregivers for dependent relatives, which makes it easier for them to remain in the family home.

DOMINICAN HOMES
Palm Leaves, Zinc, and Narco-Deco

Visitors to the country will remark on "typical Dominican homes"—charming, colorful wooden houses with zinc roofs and Victorian "gingerbread" details. While iconic and definitely photogenic, these houses are not any more "typical" than a government-issue apartment, a gleaming tower block, or a luxury mansion. In the rural areas, many people do live in simple wooden houses with zinc roofs or even palm-thatched shacks with dirt floors—usually until they can afford a more solid structure made with cement blocks. Traditional *campo* dwellings have a separate kitchen and an outdoor toilet.

With progress—and remittances from relatives who have migrated to the cities or abroad—come indoor plumbing and modern kitchens.

In some parts of the Dominican Republic, the Victorian gingerbread style has historically not been just for humble houses—the grandees of provincial capitals like Puerto Plata, Salcedo, and Montecristi lived in elegant bungalows or two-story homes built in this style.

Successive governments have rehoused people into *multi-familiares*—austerely designed apartment complexes incongruously painted in cheerful pastel colors that are often allocated to the faithful followers of the government *du jour*, rather than on the basis of need. Shared with some government buildings, this architectural style could be dubbed "tropical Stalinist."

Most middle-class people live in small houses, villas, or modern apartments. The wealthy live in luxury apartments, villas, or mansions. The *nouveau riche* live in garishly designed mansions in a style described by the *Washington Post* as "narco-deco," an allusion to the way in which many of these newly rich Dominicans are likely to have acquired their fortunes. The style is a law unto itself, but a fondness for neoclassical pastiche, improbably bright colors, and stained glass windows is a common feature.

In a general sense, the city neighborhoods are divided according to class and affluence, but there are some areas that cover the entire range, such as Arroyo Hondo in Santo Domingo; in these neighborhoods you can find mansions and shanties and everything in between. In the city center, upper-middle-class areas like Naco and Piantini are a short drive from less affluent neighborhoods like Cristo Rey and Quisqueya, and even within Naco itself there are some *barrios populares*—poor areas.

From the Country to the City

Thirty or forty years ago, 70 percent of Dominicans lived in the rural areas and 30 percent in the cities. The decline in the agricultural economy led to a dramatic level of rural-to-urban migration, however, and now the situation has been reversed. Cash crops like sugar and coffee were a mainstay of the Dominican economy until commodity prices dropped, and

the emergence of a new economic model based on tourism and free trade zones accelerated the move from rural to urban areas. Cities like Santo Domingo have grown enormously as a result, and urban planning has been haphazard, with sprawling shantytowns in many areas, most strikingly along the banks of the Ozama and Isabela rivers.

EVERYDAY LIFE

Routines vary between the city and the countryside, but there are some general patterns. The hot climate means that the day starts early.

Breakfast is usually a bread roll (*pan de agua*) and
a cup of ultra-sweet, strong black coffee or cocoa,
although the traditional hearty breakfast of
mangú con huevos/salami/queso frito (mashed
plantain or cassava with fried or scrambled eggs,
fried salami, or fried cheese) is still enjoyed
whenever possible. City streets are busy by
7:00 a.m. as people take their children to
school, which starts before 8:00 a.m. Public
transportation commuters are waiting for *guaguas*
(buses) and *carros públicos* (shared taxis), as
well as the new Santo Domingo Metro.

Office hours start at 8:00 or 9:00 a.m.,
depending on the establishment. Banks open at
9:00 or 10:00 a.m. depending on the branch, with
main branches tending to have longer hours.
Dominicans eat lunch early—in the rural areas
this can even be before noon, but the usual time
would be at about 12:00–12:30 p.m.

Work patterns and school routines have
disrupted these traditions: in the private sector
children come out of school at about 2:30 p.m.
and working parents will grab a sandwich at the
office rather than travel home for lunch as they
might have done in the past. In provincial towns
and cities everything tends to shut down from
noon to 2:00 p.m., but this is no longer the case
in the main commercial areas of the capital.

School hours last until 12:30 or 2:30 p.m., but
this varies according to school. State schools have
two or even three *tandas* (shifts) due to lack of
space: some children attend school in the
morning followed by afternoon and evening

shifts, the latter usually for mature students combining the completion of their secondary schooling with work. For this reason it is difficult to establish whether or not a child is at school— if you see children wandering the streets in the mornings it may just be that they attend the afternoon shift, not that their parents are failing to send them to school or they are playing hooky. Nonetheless, the fact remains that under-attendance levels and dropout rates are high.

Many children attend after-school activities organized by private schools, or small, private homework classrooms (*salas de tarea*) that combine day care with tutoring for children while their parents are at work.

Office hours are until around 5:00 p.m. The evening meal is usually a light affair, perhaps consisting of juice, eggs, a sandwich, or the not-so-light *mangú*.

Constant blackouts are an unfortunate feature of everyday life. Successive governments have failed to solve this chronic problem, which results from widespread electricity theft in poor neighborhoods and by certain wealthy "untouchable" consumers. To crack down on nonpayment would be political suicide for the government of the day, not to mention logistically complex. Nationalized, privatized, and joint-venture models have proved equally unsuccessful. As a result, virtually every middle- and upper-class home is equipped with a power inverter and/or an electricity generator to provide backup for outages that can last for several hours daily.

Blackouts bring economic costs to correct and stress-level costs to endure.

Tourists in large hotels equipped with massive generators are buffered from this harsh reality of life for millions of Dominicans. There are also some areas in the country (Punta Cana, Samaná, Bayahibe) serviced by independent private companies where electricity is more expensive, but reliable.

LEISURE TIME

The Dominican Republic is one of those countries where having fun is a priority, and life is seen as a constant quest for fun. The people's *joie de vivre* is palpable in the way they interact even in non-leisure situations like the workplace, and during actual leisure time the pursuit of pleasure is tackled with seriousness and determination. People will stay at home and receive visits from friends, or congregate in their *barrio* meeting points, usually a *colmado* (corner grocery store that doubles as the local watering  hole) or, in smaller towns, the central square or *parque central*. Animated conversation (known as *la chercha*) and rowdy games of dominoes, washed down with cold beers (*frías*), loud music, and spontaneous dancing, are all part of the fun.

Spectator sports (especially baseball and cockfighting) and music-related entertainment will be covered in Chapter 6.

No Smoking?

Interestingly for such a hedonistic and carefree culture, not to mention the fact that the DR is a tobacco-producing country, cigarette smoking is rare and openly frowned upon. This may surprise visitors who have been to countries like Spain and Cuba and expect to find similar customs and habits in the DR. You will seldom see Dominicans smoking in public places, especially if enclosed, to the extent that there is no need to put up smoking signs. "No smoking areas" are rare because one could say that the entire country is a smoke-free zone. The exceptions are in wealthier and foreign circles, where smoking is more common.

El Pasadía

Another popular leisure pursuit is to go on a day out, known as *un pasadía*. This consists of packing any number of family members and friends into one or more cars and heading for the beach or a river for a picnic and a swim, or to someone's house in the *campo*. Even as you go up the socioeconomic scale, the core nature of this activity does not vary that much. People still enjoy the same pursuits and only the settings will change, between poorer *campo* dwellings or popular bathing spots and sumptuous country mansions, beach houses or country clubs. This is especially popular on long weekends and comes to a climax during *Semana Santa*. Unfortunately these public holiday outings are marred by an alarming number of road accidents and drownings, and alcohol consumption undoubtedly contributes to many of these tragedies.

EVERYDAY SHOPPING

With their gleaming malls and hypermarkets, the larger cities couldn't be more cosmopolitan—a huge contrast with the untidy jumble of small-scale independent businesses that spring up in poor urban *barrios* and small provincial towns. The interesting thing is the way in which these models coexist: the upper-middle-class housewife may do her main shopping in a spotless, air-conditioned shopping mall, but will also call the local *colmado* for the items she needs there and then.

Colmados are a Dominican institution: they can be found on most street corners, even in the richest areas (albeit on a smaller scale). They sell the staples at convenience store prices and offer a motorbike home delivery service for no extra charge, although a small tip is expected. *Colmados* also serve as informal neighborhood bars, providing plastic seats and domino tables for customers as well as loud music and TV for watching sporting events.

The most popular establishments in poorer areas, after *colmados*, are hairdressing salons, *bancas* (betting shops), and small boutiques, often selling secondhand clothing sent from the USA. At the other end of the scale, Santo Domingo and Santiago have branches or franchises of many international stores like Radio Shack, Zara, Nine West, Tommy Hilfiger, and IKEA. The main supermarket chains (Supermercados Nacional, Bravo, La Sirena/Pola, La Cadena) are Dominican-owned, but there is also a PriceSmart in Santo Domingo and Santiago, and a Carrefour in Santo Domingo. A great deal of trade also takes place in the informal sector, with street-corner vendors selling snacks or fruit, and traffic-light hawkers selling phone cards, newspapers, snacks, and miscellaneous accessories.

EDUCATION

One of the main problems affecting the country is the substandard state education system. According to the UNDP Human Development Index, between 2001 and 2005 the Dominican government allocated just 1.8 percent of its GDP to education—one of the lowest percentages in Latin America and the Caribbean. This has increased in the last couple of years, but the level still falls far short of the United Nations target for education expenditure, which is 4 percent of GDP.

While there is a large private education sector, most Dominican children attend state schools. In theory at least, schooling is compulsory between the ages of five and fourteen, but in the poor rural areas especially children are pulled out of school at an early age to contribute to the family economy by working in agriculture. The grade system is like that of the USA, beginning with first grade at age six and ending with twelfth grade (or fourth year of *bachillerato*) at age eighteen. Schoolchildren take a national exam (*pruebas nacionales*) at the end of eighth grade and their baccalaureate (*bachillerato*) at the end of twelfth grade.

A large number of children do not have an official birth certificate, and this excludes many of them from attending state school. This mainly affects children of illegal Haitian immigrants, but many poor and uneducated Dominican parents simply fail to register their children's birth because of the complex bureaucratic procedure and expense involved. According to World Bank estimates, about 5 percent of Dominicans are undocumented.

The government has made some gestures toward improving the education system, recognizing in theory at least that in order to compete in a global society the country needs a skilled and literate workforce, but even with a massive injection of funds and consistent political will and commitment, any positive change is likely to come slowly. As a result, it will be a long time before many Dominicans who can afford the alternative will opt to send their children to state schools.

chapter five

MAKING FRIENDS

FRIENDSHIP BETWEEN DOMINICANS

Close friendships between Dominicans are forged in the usual places: the extended family, the neighborhood, village, or small town where people grew up, at school and at university, in sports teams and social clubs, and in the workplace.

Dominicans do not necessarily expect to be in touch with friends on a regular basis. If they run into someone whom they haven't seen for a while, even several years, the friendship will be revived. People will pull out all the stops for each other in times of need, even if contact has been lost for many years.

A typical Dominican's wider circle of friends is so vast that it could probably fill the national stadium. The word *amigo* is really an all-encompassing definition that is used to include acquaintances; in the strictest sense, friends are a more select bunch. The DR is a small country, in many ways: even in the large cities it's common for Dominicans to bump into several people they know on any given outing, and a long time is spent greeting, chatting, and catching up.

Generosity and Hospitality without Frontiers

When he was a child, my Dominican husband's family spent a couple of years living in a small town in the Cibao region. They made many friends and were much loved in the *barrio* where they lived. When he took me to visit the town, everyone remembered him and his family, even though in most cases it had been almost thirty years since they'd seen each other. It so happened that I was moving there for work, and his old neighborhood friends took me under their wing, helped me find an apartment, and opened up their homes to me, all based on my connection to their childhood friend they hadn't seen for years. (IB)

DOMINICANS AND FOREIGNERS

How easily a foreigner can break into a Dominican circle of friends depends entirely on the context. Most Dominicans will not automatically grant friendship to a foreigner: if they do they are more likely than not to be hustlers. In these situations the visitor is seen as prey, someone who is easily wooed by instant friendship, hospitality, or sexual promises from attractive women or men they would not stand a chance with in their own countries.

This is more likely to happen in hotels and other places frequented by tourists, such as the coastal resort areas and the Colonial Zone in Santo Domingo. At best, this new "friend" could end up being a helpful guide who will accompany the visitor in return for a reasonable tip, but at worst the visitor could end up being scammed and/or robbed. The usual advice about exercising caution applies, but appearing overtly suspicious is not the answer. Accepting offers of help with good humor while remaining in control by setting the boundaries is the best way to deal with it. Speaking Spanish is particularly important here: although many people in tourist areas do know some English, it is usually not enough for the subtleties involved.

In normal social settings outside the tourist areas people will also be welcoming and friendly—far beyond what many visitors from Northern countries are accustomed to. It is still advisable to exercise prudence in these situations, watching for hidden agendas, but on the whole this can be taken at face value. Visitors traveling as a couple might present fewer opportunities for misinterpretation than the lone traveler.

As we have seen, the main obstacle to engaging fully with Dominicans, their families, and their culture will be the language barrier. Even if the person speaks English, it is not a given that their entire family will do so too. In social gatherings conversation will be in Spanish, and it soon gets loud, animated, fast paced, and difficult to follow, even for non-Dominican Spanish speakers.

As well as making an effort to learn some Spanish, taking an interest in the country's culture and history, national passions like music, baseball, and dominoes, and learning to dance merengue, salsa, and bachata are other ways in which foreigners are able to cross the cultural-linguistic barrier. Deep philosophical conversations are not the norm for most Dominicans; these tend to be confined to those who are highly educated.

Experiences will also vary depending on whether the foreign visitor is older, younger, single, in a relationship, or with children.

Child-friendly Culture

Dominicans adore children, and this can be a great conversation starter. It has to be noted that the recently imposed social boundaries on engaging with other people's children in Anglo-Saxon countries especially are not usually applied in the Dominican Republic. Strangers will be physically affectionate toward children and in many cases will even offer a small child sweets and treats without consulting with the parents first. North American and northern European parents may also take a while to get used to statements like "I'm going to steal him and take him home with me" in relation to their children!

As in southern Europe, children are welcome at restaurants, even in the evenings, and are generally well behaved. Parents of babies take them out to restaurants safe in the knowledge that a staff member will happily play with their child and allow them to enjoy their meal.

A foreigner in a formal relationship with a Dominican will have a completely different experience as this is an automatic pass into the family circle and all that this entails.

MEETING PEOPLE

There is no such thing as having to break the ice with Dominicans, as there is rarely any ice to break. Dominicans are famous for being friendly, spontaneous, and welcoming. They take great pride in this national characteristic, but this does not always provide an *entrée* to their inner circle. Visitors need to beware of strangers who proffer instant friendship, especially in tourist areas—these individuals are almost always going to be hustlers. Meeting people in most other situations, however, can be rewarding and enjoyable.

Dominicans are proud of their country and are keen to show it off, and this is one way for a newcomer to build up friendships with Dominicans with whom they have come into contact. Many residents of large cities have roots in a provincial town or village, and will enjoy taking friends "home" for a weekend visit to their parents or grandparents in the *pueblo* or *campo* and the surrounding area.

Conversation can be lighthearted, with plenty of joking around, but when it becomes more serious it is very important not to be too critical about the country's shortcomings. Even if your Dominican acquaintances are fuming about some eternal problem, such as power outages, corruption, or traffic, it is best to be as diplomatic as possible—point out that these and other problems are not exclusive to the Dominican Republic, and focus on the country's positive aspects.

Enjoy the Solidarity!

I'd been a customer of the same bakery for many years. This place doubles as a community center, a place for advice, and a party political headquarters, particularly at election time. Initially the baker assumed that as an expatriate I knew nothing about Dominican politics, but when he discovered that I did my views were sought on the day's hot topic, and frequently I was questioned as to how "it" would be dealt with in my country of origin, the United Kingdom.

The day in May 2009 that the news broke about the British MPs' expenses scandal, I was met by a larger-than-usual group animatedly discussing the issue. As was to be expected, there was a great deal of glee—"See, your politicians are crooks as well!"—but what weren't expected were the genuine feelings of sadness, empathy, and solidarity that were expressed. An hour later I emerged, having used the opportunity to discuss types of community action against such evils. And I only went in to buy a loaf of bread! (GB)

Visitors who return to the DR over many years and who repeatedly meet with the same Dominicans, or expatriates who are long-term residents, may be privileged to cross the divide that exists between friendship and trust (see Chapter 2). It takes time to achieve this, and it would not be expected in the case of a first-time visitor; it is almost as though the visitor has to "earn" this position through long-term "service." Once this has happened, it is permissible to criticize negative aspects of the country, particularly the government, because you will be perceived as a fellow victim of the issue at hand.

In most situations, knowledge of Spanish is essential, the exceptions being when conversing with highly educated Dominicans who speak good English and are comfortable using it in informal situations, people who have lived in the USA, and people who work in tourist areas.

CLUBS AND ASSOCIATIONS
One way to meet Dominicans is by joining clubs. The professions (medicine, law, journalism, and so on) have their own associations, and businesspeople have organizations such as the Chambers of Commerce. There is an association of Diplomatic Wives and an International Women's Club in Santo Domingo. There are clubs for particular sports or hobbies, and members of most religions will find local congregations. In most cases the membership includes both expatriates and Dominicans, providing a first step into cultivating a social life.

SOCIALIZING WITH WORK COLLEAGUES

If you arrive from abroad to work in a Dominican environment, it is safe to say you'll receive a warm welcome from your colleagues, including invitations to socialize and to go on weekend outings. If you are invited to a colleague's home, it is nice to bring *un detallito* (a small detail) such as wine, chocolate, or a small gift, but this is not expected. A visitor may arrive empty-handed, as so often happens when the invitation is spontaneous and at short notice. The done thing in these situations is to order beers or soft drinks from the nearest *colmado* and offer to foot the bill and tip the deliveryman. Conversely, foreign residents should be aware that unannounced visits are par for the course, even in the age of the cell phone—Dominicans take such visits in stride, the common joke being that "you can always add another cup of water to the *sancocho*." Some Dominican cooks tend to prepare more food than is needed, presumably with this in mind.

If a work colleague or friend suggests going out to eat in a restaurant, the convention is that the person making the invitation will foot the bill.

SOCIALIZING WITH THE OPPOSITE SEX

Foreigners used to stiffer social conventions will be disarmed by the flirtatiousness of Dominicans—of both genders. It takes a while to learn that a compliment or a flirtatious smile is not an automatic proposition; it can be taken at

face value and accepted graciously without
having to imply anything else.
An invitation to a night out
from a colleague of the
opposite sex might involve just
that—a night out with a group of
friends, including their spouses. It is
worth establishing whether the
person making the invitation is single and
available before accepting a date.

Romance and Dating

Traditionally Dominicans do not "date" in
the North American sense. Teenage romantic
relationships involve an *enamorado*, meaning an
admirer, who if successful will go on to become
a *novio*, or boyfriend; the next steps are usually
engagement and marriage, or at least moving in
together. This process unfolds with a great deal
of family involvement, and a foreign man with
serious designs on a Dominican woman needs
to take this into account. Chaperoning on the
first few dates by her sisters, brothers, or other
family members would be the norm; it isn't
necessarily called that, but the foreign man
wondering when this "third party" will leave the
couple alone might have a long wait.

This of course refers to formal, conventional
society. In many circles, women are acquiring
more independence and may develop
relationships away from the prying eyes of
their families. This change can be linked to the

fact that most students at Dominican universities today are female.

Pay for Play

On the streets, the rules are considerably different. The Dominican Republic is well-known for its sex industry. This ranges from straightforward business transactions between men and women where money is exchanged for sex, to "relationships" where gifts and financial support are exchanged for sex and the illusion of a relationship. The latter scenario is more complicated in that it can last for months, even years, and can cause a lot of grief and pain, especially when the foreigner involved is convinced that the relationship is genuine. In these cases there are probably just as many foreign women being duped by local men, known in tourist areas as "*sanky-panky*" (a label that, somewhat improbably, is said to derive from the English "hanky-panky") as there are foreign men being duped by local women. For some poor families, bagging a foreign boyfriend or girlfriend is seen as the solution to all the family's economic woes, either in the form of regular economic support or the ultimate prize—a visa to the USA, Canada, or Europe. The DR has a high HIV rate, and not just in the tourist areas. The United Nations put it at 1.1 percent of the population in 2007 (comparable surveys put the rate in the USA at 0.6 percent, and in the UK at 0.2 percent).

This is not to say that it is impossible for foreigners and Dominicans of different socioeconomic or educational backgrounds to form genuine, long-term relationships, but it is worth exercising caution in these matters.

The Cabaña

The names given to *cabañas* are misleading. The *cabañas turísticas* that you see on the highways and on the outskirts of all towns and cities, sometimes also called "motels" or "aparthotels," are nothing of the sort. They are establishments where you can rent a room by the hour. Their standards vary from seedy and basic to opulent rococo, and are priced accordingly. A typical *cabaña* visit will involve driving into a garage with an automatic door that closes behind the car. The garage connects to a room with a bathroom. Transactions with the *cabaña* management are done through a hatch in the wall so the couple is never actually seen by the staff, for total discretion and anonymity.

These hotels are not just used by prostitutes and their clients, or for adulterous liaisons—regular couples in search of privacy and even married couples living in overcrowded conditions will sometimes go to a *cabaña*.

INVITATIONS HOME

In the *campo*, away from tourist areas, people will display a great deal of hospitality, welcoming strangers into their houses, offering coffee and insisting that you take fruit and vegetables from their gardens home with you. It is customary to accept at least a token of what is offered, bearing in mind that the coffee or "natural" fruit juice served is almost always extremely sweet.

In the city it may take a while before a Dominican will invite you to their home, but when this happens, it will usually involve a few drinks and a home-cooked meal. In some households the lady of the house will not sit down and eat with her husband and his guests: even if she has a maid, the traditional custom is for housewives to wait until everyone has eaten so she can be on standby to attend to any of her guests' needs before sitting down to her own meal. A less common traditional custom is for wives to serve their husbands and stand beside them, ensuring they have all they need, before sitting down to their own meal. This rarely takes place in younger couples.

A typical visit to a Dominican family home will involve at least drinking iced water, juice or soda, or beer, snacks like crackers, cheese, and cold cuts, and sometimes a *picadera*—a snack buffet with foods like *empanadas* and *kipes*. The customary toast is "*Salud!*" (health), with the universal clinking of glasses.

People will be invited to sit in the *galeria* (porch or balcony), especially if it is hot, or in the living room (*sala*). In rural areas, many houses have a *rancho* or gazebo for entertaining, making the most of the shade during the day and the cool night air later on. Hosts will not expect guests to be punctual and will not be taken aback if a group of friends arrives when just one or two were expected. Food is served very late, especially at a party, because it is assumed that people will leave straight after eating. Even at a small get-together couples may spontaneously get up and dance, and music is almost always played at social gatherings.

GRINGOS CAN'T DANCE

Some Dominicans are cosmopolitan and well-traveled enough to distinguish between foreigners of different types and nationalities. Those who have never left the island will have a more limited perception, often lumping all foreigners in the category of *Americanos* and attributing very generalized characteristics to all foreigners. In tourist areas, locals will have obtained a more firsthand image of foreigners and their quirks, but these will also be one-dimensional in that the tourists these locals have encountered will often be those who have been warned that all Dominicans are out to rip them off, and who behave accordingly. As is the nature of tourist areas everywhere in the world, there are real hustlers who see foreigners as a meal ticket or, as the song goes, a *"visa para un sueño"*—a visa to a dream.

The Concept of Aplatanado

Aplatanado comes from the word *plátano*—plantain, the quintessentially Dominican staple food. A foreigner who adapts to the country is said to have become "like a plantain," or *aplatanado*. This compliment is not handed out lightly. To qualify for the honor, you have to speak Spanish like a local, eat Dominican food—or even better, learn to cook it—dance like a native, play dominoes, and hold your own during an animated Dominican *chercha*.

chapter six

TIME OUT

Free time is not in short supply in a country where
unemployment and underemployment are high. In
the poorest sectors especially, it is common for one
or two working adults to support a large extended
clan, often from afar. As a result, many people have
a lot of time on their hands, and some spend it
playing dominoes or chatting to neighbors, usually
out in the open air. Across the social spectrum,
people in regular employment also place great
emphasis on their leisure time and make a point
of enjoying it to the fullest. Dominicans are not
solitary creatures: leisure is usually pursued
collectively, with family, friends, and neighbors.

MUSIC AND DANCING
Music and dancing are an integral part of
Dominican life. Even a small child's birthday party
will involve loud music pumping out—most
Dominicans find it inconceivable that a social
gathering could take place without loud and lively
musical accompaniment. Dancing venues are
everywhere, but given the chance, most
Dominicans will dance anywhere—at home,
outside the *colmado*, and at the car wash.

To some extent, a person's background and age will determine their taste in music. Traditionalists and older people will opt for Puerto Rican salsa, Cuban *son*, and the Dominican people's own *merengue tipico*, as played by *perico ripiao* trios (grater, drum, accordion, maracas, and bass); merengue has moved with the times, and each subsequent

generation has molded the style to its tastes.

Popular groups of the day perform at large-scale, government-organized street parties in places like Santo Domingo's Malecón on special occasions such as Christmas, New Year, Carnival, and the capital's merengue festival, attended by thousands of people.

Bachata is the country music of the Dominican Republic, with its roots in bolero. It has managed to cross over to the mainstream and is much loved by visitors. It is bittersweet, sentimental, and melancholic, and like the Argentinean tango it originated in lowlife dives and brothels. Several performers like the young Dominican–American group Aventura have updated bachata and taken it to an international audience. Nonetheless, many urban Dominicans still look down on bachata as hick, low-class music. Its main exponents are Antony Santos, Raulín Rodríguez, and Monchy y Alexandra.

The Story of Merengue

This quintessentially Dominican dance and musical genre, so the story goes, evolved during colonial times after African servants watched their masters dancing European-style polkas and waltzes at their parties, and adapted it to their own rhythms. It is true that merengue includes elements of European dance, such as accordion music and dancing in pairs. Merengue languished on the fringes of society until Trujillo brought it into the mainstream. Classical merengue artists of these years were Joseito Mateo, Luis Alberti, and the Orquesta Santa Cecilia.

In the 1970s and 1980s musicians like Johnny Ventura, Wilfrido Vargas, and Fernando Villalona adapted the sound to the times with a slicker, big-band style featuring wind sections and keyboards. In the 1990s, Jose Pena Suazo's Banda Gorda and Los Hermanos Rosario gave merengue a more streetwise, techno sound, and in the 2000s Omega continued this trend with his urban merengue. However, it was Juan Luis Guerra who brought merengue to a truly international audience from the late 1980s onward, with his catchy, pop-influenced arrangements and intelligent, satirical lyrics. Difficult to categorize but of great importance in the evolution of merengue is Luis Dias, in terms of fusion as well as rediscovering its folkloric roots.

Reggaeton comes from Puerto Rico and is very popular indeed with young Dominicans. Ibiza-style electronic music and European DJs have a huge following in the DR, mainly among the urban middle classes. Dominicans of all ages love rock music, both classic and contemporary. While some big-name rock stars like Sting and Santana have performed in the country in recent years, more common are visits by has-beens and tribute bands.

Music venues range from the rough-and-ready *disco-terrazas* in the rural areas to sophisticated clubs in the large cities with a strict—some say racist—door policy. The usual excuse given is that the establishment has a dress code. Investigative journalists have put this to the test and proved that nightclub staff have denied darker-skinned customers entrance on the grounds that the club is hosting a private party, only to let in lighter-skinned customers later on that same evening.

Young Dominicans of all classes also enjoy congregating around certain spots, like the Malecón, Avenida del Puerto, and Lincoln Avenue in the capital, buying beer and snacks from street vendors, and blasting music out of their cars.

Nueva canción (new song), also known as *nueva trova* (new troubadours) in Cuba, is a popular Latin American musical style that consists mainly of melodic ballads, sometimes with a political/protest theme. Dominican singers in this tradition include Pavel Nuñez, Victor Victor, and Sonia Silvestre.

Some Dominican city-based rock musicians like Roldán Marmol and Xiomara Fortuna have rediscovered and nurtured marginal traditional folkloric *gagá*, *Fiesta de Palo*, and *salve* musicians and recorded roots fusion-type music with them, bringing their music to a mainstream audience.

The Musical Class Divide

I once accompanied a British rock star on a visit to rural areas of the DR. The musician was the spokesman for a particular campaign, and part of the publicity work involved his commenting on the realities of life for poor Dominican farmers. In a mountain village he met teenagers who had clearly never heard of him or any other non-Spanish artists. Later that day he was interviewed by a Santo Domingo radio station and discovered that his group's latest release was at the number one slot of that week's playlist, massively popular with middle-class, urban Dominicans. (IB)

Jazz has a strong following in certain circles and there are annual jazz festivals in Puerto Plata and at Casa de Teatro in the capital. Grammy-winning Dominican jazz pianist Michael Camilo has had success on a global level.

The classical music and ballet scene appeals to a more limited sector, with a year-round program of performances and concerts by national and international musicians and dancers, mainly at Santo Domingo's National Theater, Santiago's Gran Teatro del Cibao, and Altos de Chavon amphitheater near La Romana. There is a National Symphony Orchestra and a National Ballet.

DOMINICAN CUISINE

Dominicans love their traditional food, and although they have adopted several international dishes and enjoy eating food from other countries, they remain fiercely loyal to their home-cooked cuisine.

There's more to Dominican food than just rice and beans: other favorites include breakfast standard *mangú*—pureed plantains served with fried onions, scrambled eggs, fried cheese, or fried salami. Family get-togethers are an excuse to make a *sancocho*—a hearty stew with several types of meat, tubers, vegetables, and herbs, washed down with several icy *frías* (beers) and often followed by an animated game of dominoes in the shade of a mango tree.

Regional variations include fish in coconut sauce in the Samaná area, goat stew from the northwest (one of the few spicy dishes on the national menu), *chen-chen*, which is similar to polenta, in the southwest, and Middle Eastern-influenced dishes like *tipile* (tabbouleh) and *kipes* (*kibbes*) from the southeast.

There are also seasonal dishes, like the uniquely Dominican sweet beans at Easter and roast pork for Christmas Eve dinner.

Favorite Dominican alcoholic drinks, besides beer and rum, include whiskey and vodka and cranberry. Natural fruit juices—especially passion fruit (*chinola*), papaya (*lechoza*), orange (*china* or *naranja*), and tamarind (*tamarindo*)—are served in many places, but foreigners will almost always find them oversweetened. Interesting concoctions include *champola*, made with soursop (*guanabaná*), and *morir soñando*—literally, "to die dreaming"—which is made with fresh orange juice, ice, condensed milk, and a hefty dose of sugar.

The Dominican Republic produces excellent coffee, and while in many other coffee-growing countries the best stuff is reserved for export, in the DR local brands like Café Santo Domingo are perfectly drinkable. There are also some better, premium alternatives including organic Monte Alto. Dominicans drink coffee black, strong, and unbelievably sweet. Other hot beverages loved by Dominicans are ginger tea (*te de jengibre*) and hot chocolate prepared without milk.

Plato del Día

The standard Dominican lunch is known as *la bandera* (the flag), as its three main components supposedly represent the red (beans), white (rice), and blue (meat!) that make up the country's flag. Most Dominican homes traditionally serve this every single lunchtime, accompanied by salad. As well as red kidney or pinto beans, Dominicans love black beans. The meat component can be chicken, pork, beef, or fish. The best place to sample *la bandera* is at a Dominican home, a popular neighborhood *comedor* (sometimes called a *cafeteria económica*) catering to workers, or a more formal restaurant specializing in Dominican food, like Adrian Tropical in the capital.

EATING OUT

Dominicans are great lovers of home-cooked food, and many would prefer a family get-together at home or in the *campo* to a restaurant outing. At the same time, dining out is growing in popularity, and this is reflected in the burgeoning number of restaurants of all types and price ranges. Conventions for restaurant etiquette vary according to the type of establishment, but in most cases visitors may do as they would do at home. The universal signals for summoning a waiter and asking for the bill are understood, although some Dominicans may use a "pssst" sound for this purpose.

A truly cosmopolitan selection of restaurants can be found only in the two main cities, Santo Domingo and Santiago, and in the touristy areas. Most provincial towns will have a pizzeria and a Chinese restaurant, but the only other options will be the Dominican standard lunchtime *plato del día* or *pica pollo* (fried chicken). In contrast, Santo Domingo has dozens of good-quality restaurants serving almost every conceivable style of food. For example, in recent years Dominicans have discovered the delights of sushi, and there are several sushi bars around the city, ranging from the cheap and cheerful to the overpriced and sophisticated. Italian, Spanish, Chinese, Mexican, Brazilian, Argentinean, and fusion cuisine are also easy to find.

Special Dietary Needs
Vegetarian options are relatively easy to find in the two main cities, whether at mainstream restaurants serving nonmeat dishes or specialist vegetarian restaurants like Ananda in Gazcue and Govinda in Zona Universitaria. Kosher and halal meat is less easy to come by, although information on this may be obtained from the Jewish and

Muslim communities in Santo Domingo. Health food shops in the capital sell gluten-free products, and the larger supermarkets have specialist/health food aisles. The advent of more expatriates living on the north coast has seen better provision of sugar-free jams, cookies, and other products—doubtless due to customer demand, since the taste buds of many foreigners cannot adapt to the Dominican love of sugar.

TIPPING

Leaving a tip in restaurants is optional, and Dominicans as a rule do not leave much beyond the 26 percent tax and service charge added to most restaurant bills. Only a minority of establishments include it in their menu prices. It is recommended to leave 10% on top of the total, however, and if paying by credit card, to leave the tip in cash. Beyond restaurants, tipping is not expected in most places. Porters and bellhops will expect two or three dollars. Tour guides should also be tipped. Taxi drivers should only be rewarded if they perform some extra task.

Street Food

This is not the healthiest option, and the unacclimatized visitor should approach with caution, but fried snacks sold on the streets are much loved by Dominicans. Typical street foods are *yaniqueques* (Johnny cakes), *pastelitos* and *empanadas* (meat or cheese-filled pasties), *chimichurris* (burgers), and *kipes* (Middle Eastern meat patties or *kibbes*), most of which are also standard fare for buffets at parties. As if to balance this out, fresh fruit is also a popular street food—vendors will peel and slice it and serve in a plastic bag or Styrofoam tray, or you can buy the fruit whole and peel it yourself.

CULTURAL LIFE

Dominican art ranges from the folkloric and popular, exemplified by stylized oils depicting rural scenes of peasant houses and flamboyant trees in bloom, to cutting-edge installation art. Acclaimed painters include Yoryi Morel, Silvano Lora, Ivan Tovar, Guillo Perez, and Ramon Oviedo. Cándido Bidó is active in bringing art therapy to the DR's prison system. Camilo Sestero is a prolific painter, and his expressionistic interpretations of Dominican and other themes are popular. Groundbreaking younger artists include Raquel Paiewonsky and Iris Perez.

Locations are the Museum of Modern Art in the Plaza de la Cultura, Museo Bellapart, Centro León in Santiago, smaller galleries in the Colonial Zone, and the Casa de Teatro. The Casa de Cultura in Puerto Plata hosts many art and photographic exhibitions as well as being a popular venue for book launches.

There are some impressive murals around the city; these date mainly from the mid-twentieth century, when the genre was at its height across Latin America. Many public buildings that date back to the Trujillo years feature the work of Vela Zannetti, a Spanish muralist who settled in the DR along with a sizeable community of Spanish artists and intellectuals opposed to the Franco regime. In the center of Puerto Plata, local group Arte 48 have transformed the outside of the old court building with murals.

Photography is very popular as an art form as well as being a form of social/political expression.

There is an active theater scene, musicals are staged at the Teatro Nacional and the Gran Teatro del Cibao, and smaller productions can be seen in fringe venues such as  the Teatro las Mascaras, Teatro Guloya, and Casa de Teatro in the capital.

As well as large multiplexes screening Hollywood blockbusters, there is also a Cinematheque showing alternative cinema in Santo Domingo. There is a small but active local cinema industry, and most Dominican movies of the last few years have been in the comedy genre: *Perico Ripiao*, *Sanky-Panky*, and *Ladrones a Domicilio*. More serious issues were tackled in *La Victoria*, a film about jails, and one horror film—*Andrea*.

SPORTS AND EXERCISE

The Dominican Republic is a sports-loving nation in every sense. Dominicans are passionate as both spectators and participants in sports, especially baseball. There is also a trend toward sports for personal fitness and health as well as recreation.

Gyms are becoming popular, with state-of-the-art installations springing up in the large cities. One of the main forms of fitness exercise is walking, and in the early mornings and evenings walkers take to the streets, parks, and seafront boulevards. Running and cycling are also popular.

Introduced by invading US forces in the early twentieth century, baseball is the DR's national sport. Today dozens of Dominicans play in the Major Leagues. Dominicans fervently follow

national and US baseball, and many young boys strive for a Major League career. Several US teams have special baseball academies in the DR for training these prospects.

As far as other team sports go, basketball and soccer are also played, but not nearly on the same scale, and even rugby and American football make an appearance. In recent years a group of cricket fans have set up the Dominican Cricket Association. Golf is popular with Dominicans, and many foreign visitors come to play on the famous Dominican courses.

While they are not exactly sports, cockfighting and lively games of dominoes are enjoyed by Dominicans of all classes.

SHOPPING FOR PLEASURE

Going to the mall is a relatively new phenomenon, but the attraction of these air-conditioned spaces is understandable, especially on a sweltering summer's day. Visitors may appreciate the more folksy appeal of Calle El Conde pedestrianized mall in Santo Domingo's Colonial Zone, and the streets of the Colonial Zone in general. As well as crafts, items to look out for are world-class Dominican cigars, rum, and coffee.

Crafts

Once you get past all the globalized junk produced in Asian factories and labeled as souvenirs of the Dominican Republic, there is a range of genuine locally handcrafted items available in souvenir shops. This includes Taíno-influenced paintings, wall hangings, ceramics, artifacts such as those produced by the Guillén Brothers cooperative in Yamasá, the traditional "faceless doll" statues, and amber and larimar (an endemic, pale blue semiprecious stone) jewelry. Dominican artists such as Antonio Guadalupe produce affordable versions of their artwork.

TOP ATTRACTIONS

While Dominicans have long been proud of their country's history, culture, and beauty, they have only started to engage in active internal tourism in recent years—possibly as a consequence of seeing millions of foreign visitors marveling at what the Dominicans themselves perhaps took for granted.

Going to the beaches at Easter and seeking relief from the year-round heat by swimming in the rivers, waterfalls, and natural pools has always been popular, but Dominicans are also starting to realize the value of what they have on their doorstep. More and more locals now go trekking up Pico Duarte in January, whale watching in February, and heading for the cooler climes of the central mountains in summer—all previously the domain of tourists,

As well as the beaches for which it is famous, the DR has a range of exceptional cultural and ecotourism attractions.

Santo Domingo

The capital, with its palm-lined seafront avenue known as the Malecón, is located on the south coast of the island. Santo Domingo has a lot going for it, although it cannot be denied that it suffers from all the usual big-city problems of air pollution, traffic congestion, and a moderate level of street crime.

The historic Colonial Zone, currently undergoing renovation and restoration by UNESCO, dates back to the fifteenth century, with colonial and even art deco architecture (notable ruins include the first European-built hospital in the Americas) and plenty of scope for people watching, soaking in the atmosphere, indulging in gastronomy, and souvenir shopping.

The modern city also has its charms, with a vibrant cosmopolitan atmosphere, world-class botanical gardens, a range of museums, art galleries, mega shopping malls, and an active cultural scene and sophisticated nightlife.

Further Afield

The DR's provincial towns and cities should not be overlooked. These include the north coast city of Puerto Plata, where tourists and busloads of local schoolchildren line up to take the cable car up Mount Isabel de Torres to the Botanical Gardens, with sweeping views over the city and coastline. Puerto Plata's many attractions include houses built in the Victorian "gingerbread" style, a sixteenth-century Spanish fort, and a

seafront boulevard, along with the color, noise, chaos, and bustle found in every Dominican city.

Other cities of interest to visitors include Samaná, Sosúa, Salcedo, Montecristi, Jarabacoa, San José de Ocoa, La Romana, and the country's second city, Santiago de los Caballeros.

Archaeology

Archaeology and history buffs will appreciate the the ruins of the DR's first European settlement at La Isabela (north coast), an early colonial sugar plantation at Nigua (near Santo Domingo), and the abandoned city of La Vega Vieja (center). Going further back in time, there is an indigenous stone circle, Corral de los Indios, in San Juan de la Maguana (southwest), and Taíno petroglyphs in caves such as Cueva de Las Maravillas (southeast) and Los Haitises (northeast).

Carnival

Carnival takes place throughout February in most major towns and cities, with a national parade in Santo Domingo featuring the best troupes selected from all the regional carnivals. This is very much a Dominican celebration, as opposed to an event staged for the benefit of tourists. While visitors are guaranteed to enjoy the spectacle, some of the traditional and topical in-jokes will inevitably go over their heads.

Natural Attractions

Whale watching takes place every February, when humpback whales from the North Atlantic

migrate to the Bay of Samaná (northeast) to
mate and give birth to their calves.

National parks include the mangroves and
caves of Los Haitises (northeast), the stark,
semiarid beauty of Bahia de las Aguilas and Lago
Enriquillo (southwest), the idyllic white sands of
Isla Saona (off the southeast coast), and the
Central Highlands, with the highest peak in the
Caribbean, Pico Duarte. El Limon waterfall
(Samaná) and the Jarabacoa and Constanza areas
(central mountains) are just three destinations for
hiking, swimming, and river sports.

"One Thousand Miles of Beaches"
The DR's legendary beaches are what really put the
country on the map as a mass tourist destination.
Along with the deserted, white-sand, palm-fringed
beaches of the tourist brochures, visitors will also
find crowded, bustling beaches favored by locals
(Boca Chica), tourist beaches with all the water
sports you can think of, and a few more for good
measure (Punta Cana, North Coast, Bayahibe), and

completely virgin beaches with few or no amenities (Samaná, northeast; Punta Rucia and El Morro de Montecristi, northwest; beaches in the southwest).

While most foreign visitors come to enjoy the beaches with a drink and a good book, interspersed with an occasional burst of activity in the shape of water sports, the Dominicans descend on the beaches en masse to enjoy each other's company and to party—the peak season for this is Easter week.

Although officially all beaches are public, this is not the case in practice, and some of the best beaches are now within the limits of exclusive tourist and residential developments. Nonetheless, there is still a reasonable degree of public access to beaches in all areas of the country. Highlights are the beaches known for extreme wind sports in Cabarete (north) and Salinas (southwest), the mostly deserted white sands of Samaná (northeast), and tourist beaches—both relaxing and lively—along the east, north, and south coasts.

For information, visit the official government tourist site at www.godominicanrepublic.com, or the highly recommended site www.dr1.com.

chapter seven

TRAVEL, HEALTH, & SAFETY

The Dominican Republic's transport infrastructure is a work in progress. Generally speaking the main highways connecting the large cities are kept in good condition, while roads connecting smaller towns have an ample supply of potholes and other hazards, may become impassable after heavy rains, and are sometimes washed out completely. In the last ten years successive governments have constructed or renovated many highways, bridges, tunnels, and overpasses.

Highways connect Santo Domingo with the rest of the country. The three most important ones are the DR-1, known as the Autopista Duarte, which goes from Santo Domingo northwest to Santiago and Montecristi; the DR-2, which goes west to Comendador; and the DR-3, known as the Autopista del Este, which links to the east of the island. Recently the eagerly awaited Carretera de Samaná has vastly reduced driving time to the Samaná peninsula. Drivers of private vehicles can expect to pay tolls on these highways; for passengers on public buses, these are already covered by the fare.

ROAD TRAVEL
Long-distance Buses
Long-distance public transportation is fast, modern, reliable, inexpensive—and freezing cold! This is more than compensated for by the warmth and friendliness of one's fellow travelers, however. Take the Metro bus for the three-and-a-half-hour journey from Puerto Plata to Santo Domingo and you will know more than you need to about the marriage of the person sitting next to you. Likewise, if you have brought snacks for the journey, the expectation would be that you would offer these around; some people might pass round a bottle of rum. Party time! For a writer or people watcher, this culture is the richest of resources.

Both Metro and Caribe Tours buses have their air-conditioning controls preset; entreaties to the drivers, while heard with empathy, will result in no action, so take a jacket or sweater and a pair of socks. Metro and Caribe run frequent services between the major cities: for example, half-hourly or hourly Metro services run between Santiago and Santo Domingo depending on the time of day, and there are eight services daily from Puerto Plata to Santo Domingo. The fare for the nearly four-hour journey from Puerto Plata to Santo Domingo is around US$10, and Metro allows booking in advance. Further information can be found at www.caribetours.com.do and www.metroserviciosturisticos.com.

City Buses
City buses are usually older, with the only air-conditioning provided by the absence of window panes. Rates are inexpensive; they depend on duration of journey, but are usually less than US$1 for trips within the city. Outside Santo Domingo and Santiago there are no bus stops as such, but everyone knows the usual stopping places—everyone, that is, apart from the visitor! Santo Domingo and Santiago are served by the state public transportation system (OMSA), with large buses, some air-conditioned, serving set routes with formal bus stops.

How to Flag Down a Bus

Look for a gathering of people by the side of the road: it will mean a traffic accident, a political caravan giving away freebies prior to election time, or a recognized stopping point for public transportation. Failing that, stand near the roadside; usually a form of public transportation will find *you*, but if not, raise a finger in an almost imperceptible gesture to the approaching vehicle. The convention is that a finger pointed to the ground indicates a short journey, while one pointed forward in the air indicates a long journey (long-haul services may not stop for short journeys). Those waving hands, arms, or whole body are clearly foreigners who have yet to learn the subtleties of the Dominican gesturing system—or have just been bitten by something! In Santo Domingo and Santiago each route has its own special gesture, so a crash course from a local is necessary before venturing out.

Guaguas or Voladoras

Guaguas (pronounced "wag-was"), also known as *voladoras*, are an informal network of privately owned minibuses and vans in various stages of repair that span the entire country and serve as the lifeblood of Dominican transportation. Linking virtually every area of the island, they are especially vital in the remote countryside where the intercity buses do not run. Generally speaking, they are not air-conditioned and are often quite cramped. *Guaguas* feature both a driver and a *cobrador*, who hangs out of the door and yells out the bus's destination—don't expect to hear much English spoken. The *cobrador* will take your fare, usually on completion of the journey. A typical half-hour journey between Puerto Plata and Sosúa will cost approximately US $1.10. The same journey by private taxi would be US $27.

How to Get Off a Bus or Guagua

When you're ready to get off, shout out to the driver, "*Dejame aquí!*" ("Let me off here!") or (phonetically) "*Keena, keena*," and make your way quickly to the exit. *Keena* represents the word *esquina* (the corner), with, in Dominican pronunciation, the "s" being silent, which means the "e" disappears as well. Any loud noise will suffice in lieu of the Spanish language, and fellow passengers will usually help to get the message across.

Taxis

There are two types of taxi—those for personal use, and those for public use. Public taxis, also known as *conchos* or *públicos*, pick up passengers in the same way as *guaguas*, are similarly inexpensive, and feature seating arrangements that bear little resemblance to the vehicle manufacturer's specifications. *Público* drivers may pack two passengers in the front seat and four in the back, regardless of the size of the car. It is possible to pay two fares and book exclusivity for the front seat, or pay four fares and get the back seat. Journeys cost about 60 cents. Taxis in the DR do not have meters; fares are fixed, and tipping is not expected.

Tourist Taxis or Local Taxis

Private taxis will have different rates depending on whether they are tourist taxis or those used by locals. Journeys within Santo Domingo cost just over US $4 for the latter. The same distance on the north coast by a taxi based at a tourist hotel would be US $15. Tourist taxis have fixed rates for journeys, and these are usually posted at hotels and airports. Tipping is not expected unless the driver has performed the services of a tour guide. Residents tend to use local taxi companies like Tecni-Taxi or Apolo. A list of taxi companies for Santiago and Santo Domingo can be found at www.taxird.com.

Motoconchos

Motoconchos are motorcycles that ply for hire. These are inexpensive, but not the safest form of transport. The passenger sits on the bike and clutches on to either the driver or the seat. Older women may even sit sidesaddle to preserve their modesty and in inclement weather open an umbrella over themselves and the driver. Attempts have been made to regulate the *motoconchos*, but adherence to transit laws is not high on many of the drivers' agendas. A twenty-minute journey from one side of Puerto Plata to the other costs

US $2. A recent regulation mandates the use of helmets for drivers, but not for passengers—old habits die hard, however, so drivers' helmets can often be seen swinging from the handlebars. In keeping with the importance of interpersonal relationships in the DR, drivers often look from side to side and wave greetings to acquaintances; indeed, the only person staring fixedly ahead to spot oncoming problems might be the passenger.

Car Rental

There are many rental car companies, but it is safer to rent from reputable firms like National, Avis, Hertz, or Budget, all of which have online facilities for prebooking and car collection from most of the larger airports. These companies all provide backup in the event of a breakdown, while some of the smaller ones might not; some of the less reputable rental companies have also been known to make creative use of credit cards!

A Word about Driving

Amazingly, there are fewer accidents than one might expect, given the general disregard for traffic regulations, the fact that a high proportion of drivers do not possess licenses (many who do may have bought them rather than passed a test), and the ability of the locals to find things to concentrate on other than the road ahead. The visitor needs to drive defensively without assuming that anyone else is using mirrors. Up until 2007 there was no law banning alcohol and driving; this is now in place but is implemented sporadically, and although thousands of breathalyzers have been imported, it is rare to see such a test being applied.

If visitors are stopped by police, they should first check that the individuals stopping them actually are police officers and not imposters. The transit police, AMET (*Autoridad Metropolitana de Transporte*), wear green uniforms and have the authority to stop drivers for traffic infractions. The *Policía Nacional*, in gray, also have the authority to search vehicles for drugs or guns. Neither has the authority to stop vehicles and ask for money, but it happens. Visitors who comply could be targeted the next day and the day after that, so it's best not to; if you demonstrate no understanding of Spanish, you are likely to be waved on. Carry all car documents, a copy of your driver's license, and copies of your passport. Under no circumstances should you hand over originals; AMET are not authorized to retain original licenses.

RAIL

Most of the DR's railways were built to service
the sugar mills, and not as a passenger service.
President Fernández introduced an underground
and overground mass transit system known as the
Metro in Santo Domingo in 2008, and the service
went into operation at the end of January 2009.
The service links suburbs such as Villa Mella with
the Centro de los Heroes, passing through
Maximo Gomez, La Zurza, Gazcue, and Ciudad
Universitaria. There are also plans for a second
Metro line in Santo Domingo and a light rail
service connecting the port of Haina with
Santiago, the DR's second-largest city and one
which has a busy free zone industrial area. The
Metro has long been the butt of political cartoons
focusing on the needs of a country with poor
educational and health facilities. A one-way ride
costs RD $30; a rechargeable Metro card must be
purchased at the cost of RD $30. This card,

available at any Metro station, must be charged with a minimum of RD $30 and can be charged with a maximum of RD $1,000.

DOMESTIC FLIGHTS

A number of private air companies such as Air Century, Volair, Aerodomca, and SAPair offer flights linking domestic and international airports within the DR. The most popular routes are those linking Punta Cana, Samaná, Santo Domingo, La Romana, and Puerto Plata. There are both scheduled and private charter flights and business executive services, but the economic recession of 2009 has resulted in many companies cutting back on their scheduled services; Web sites have not necessarily been changed accordingly, so a telephone call or e-mail contact in advance is advised. Further information can be found at www.colonialtours.com.do/vuelos/vuelos.asp.

Sol Dominicana Airlines ceased operating in 2009, and Caribair was ordered by the Dominican Civil Aviation Institute to cease operations for one year in January 2009 because of "masking multiple commercial operations as private operations in unauthorized airplanes." Caribair announced that it would appeal against this decision, and its Web site remains unaltered. The suspension was lifted by the Dominican Civil Aviation Institute on June 12, 2009, and Caribair resumed service with a limited number of aircraft and pilots.

HEALTH

The public health sector is woefully under-resourced. This means it is not uncommon for surgeons to finish operations by the light of their cell phones when the power goes off and insufficient funding means no fuel for the generator. Dominican citizens frequently have to provide supplies used in surgical procedures.

In contrast, in the private sector there are state-of-the-art facilities such as Hospital Metropolitano de Santiago in Santiago, the CEDIMAT (Centro de Diagnostico, Medicina Avanzada, Conferencias Medicas y Telemedicina) Plaza de la Salud in Santo Domingo (www.cedimat.com), Clinica Abreu in Santo Domingo (www.clinicaabreu.com.do), and on the east coast, Hospiten Bávaro (www.hospiten.es).

On the north coast a new private hospital, Centro Medico Cabarete, opened in Sosúa in July 2009, and in Puerto Plata the Centro Médico Bournigal (www.bournigal-hospital.com), while not state-of-the-art, offers an acceptable service. Where possible it is advisable to seek a recommendation for a surgeon from a trusted source. Patients are generally expected to settle their bills before leaving the hospital and file a claim with their insurers later. Permission to leave may not be given until dues are met; this stems from the experience of previous visitors who did not pay their bills.

Hospital care requiring an overnight stay is a family matter, with family members coming in to the hospital to care for their relative. Lone travelers can overcome this lack by giving a thoughtful present to underpaid and overworked nurses in exchange for more care than would be the norm. Intensive care facilities tend to have the same level of care available in affluent Western countries.

No Peace for the Sick!

If a patient enters a hospital in the DR, it is assumed that their family will undertake much of the nursing duties and will stay with them overnight. Most private clinics have a spare divan in the patient's room for this purpose. To the foreigner, these gatherings can seem more like social events than aids to recovery. Indeed, even sickness at home in the privacy of one's own bed might not be the peaceful scenario hoped for: the social obligation to visit the sick means a constant supply of well-wishers!

Many of the tourist resorts have a medical center onsite or nearby, and for serious issues within the hotel, staff will call a doctor to visit. There are many doctors and surgeons who speak some English. Patients may be sent to a laboratory for tests; results are usually available quite quickly.

The sort of ailments most likely to be suffered will not require hospital treatment and can be minimized greatly with preventative measures:

mosquito repellent to avoid malaria or dengue fever, for example. Before leaving home visitors should discuss with their doctors pills or vaccinations for malaria, meningitis, and hepatitis. Strong sunscreen should be used to prevent sunburn. Keeping hydrated is important in tropical temperatures, so plenty of water and juice should be consumed; alcohol tends to dehydrate. Tap water should be avoided in the DR. Some visitors find their stomachs react to the laxative affects of the coconut oil that is often used in cooking; Prodom (Imodium) is available at pharmacies, but visitors may wish to bring some with them.

Dental tourism is beginning to make its mark on the DR, where tourists combine a holiday with specific treatments. Prices are far lower than could be expected in certain first-world countries: a root canal, post, and crown, for example, costs about US $530. Dental implants cost US $850 per implant, plus a further US $400 for the crown.

SAFETY

In common with the rest of the Caribbean, much of Latin America, and indeed, the rest of the world, crime and particularly that associated with the narcotics trade is now a fact of life in the DR.

For the most part, however, this affects residents, Dominican and expatriate alike, and not tourists. Even criminals are aware that income from tourism is crucial to the wealth of the DR. Nevertheless, travelers should remain alert and be aware of their surroundings.

Certain commonsense rules apply: not wearing an excess of gold jewelry; only carrying sufficient cash for the day's needs; not displaying a wallet stuffed full of bills in public; not wandering off the beaten path alone on foot; not leaving valuables visible in a parked car; using a "fanny pack" for valuables rather than a shoulder-strap handbag; not mixing with prostitutes or their pimps in tourist areas; and for men, carrying wallets in front rather than rear pockets.

Watch your Rear!

Prostitutes often diversify their talents and are gifted pickpockets. An unknown woman climbing all over you in a display of "affection" should be viewed with suspicion, and with the hand instantaneously covering the wallet pocket. Some pickpockets wait until the intended victim is at a disadvantage: male visitors using the urinal in some tourist bars might be surprised by a female pickpocket approaching from behind when both his hands are occupied. Either leave your wallet with your traveling companion or have someone watch your rear!

The vast majority of tourists have an incident-free, thoroughly enjoyable holiday. Crimes such as kidnapping tourists for ransom are virtually unknown, and the worst thing that is likely to happen is paying a tad too much for an item you were purchasing because your negotiation skills were not sufficiently honed.

The services of a "guide" will be offered everywhere in tourist areas; there are official, uniformed guides, and employing one of these will keep the others, official and unofficial, at bay. As we will see in Chapter 9, body language is important here: purposeful, confident pedestrians will avoid setting themselves up as a target in a tourist area.

Problems with crime are far less noticeable in non-tourist areas. Some travelers (and residents) have reported problems with ATM machines—card information theft, for example—and it is always advisable to enter the bank during banking hours and withdraw cash from a teller.

If problems do occur, it should be remembered that many of the police are corrupt as well as underpaid, and can view a foreigner with difficulties as an opportunity to "earn." This is more likely to be the case in tourist areas than non-tourist areas.

Visitors are advised to be aware of their embassy Web site and location. Most embassies are in Santo Domingo, but there is also consular representation for many nationalities on the north, northeast, and east coasts.

No visitor should even contemplate buying drugs in the DR; penalties are harsh, and the prisons are very third world. The corruption level of some police, themselves involved in the narco-industry, should not be mistaken as a sign of leniency toward such crimes. In fact, it is better not to even have a conversation about drugs unless you know with whom you are speaking— it could be an undercover cop!

chapter eight

BUSINESS BRIEFING

BUSINESS CULTURE

Dominicans are gifted entrepreneurs. The types of businesses in the DR range from large multinational companies and large national companies owned by well-known Dominican families right across the spectrum to one-man-band enterprises such as the street seller with a mobile food cart. Clearly business protocol and etiquette will vary with the type of company, and the practices of the multinational companies will be much like corporate protocol in the USA and Europe.

What's in a Name?

For starters, it is worth doing a little research to ensure that your company name does not, of itself, give cause for offense or misunderstanding —foreign marketing in Latin America has a history of "whoops" moments. Frank Perdue's famous slogan "It takes a tough man to make a tender chicken" was plastered on billboards across Mexico in a translation that amounted to "It takes a hard man to make a chicken affectionate." In the DR, the Japanese bathroom product manufacturer Toto has faced marketing issues—

toto is Dominican slang for a certain part of the female anatomy.

Since the advice would always be to have your business card printed on both sides, in English on one side and Spanish on the other, and to present the Spanish side uppermost, it is well worth checking with a Dominican that your company name or logo does not undermine your endeavors right from the get-go.

PERSONAL RELATIONSHIPS AND NETWORKING

Dominicans set great store by interpersonal relationships, as would be expected in a collectivist culture. Networking is an important part of business since it broadens your base of contacts, and therefore, people who can smooth the way for you. The DR is a country where who you  know is often more important than what you know; Dominican professionals go to great lengths to network, making extensive use of social networking Web sites and even sending their children to schools where the parents will meet the "right" people. Even leisure activities can be focused for business advantage: joining the right yacht or golf club, for example.

For the foreign businessperson, behaving in a culturally acceptable manner—being seen as a foreigner who, if not yet, is almost "one of us"—

can make the difference between winning and losing a deal. Your product might be inferior to that of another foreigner, but if your competitor is perceived by the Dominican client as uptight, cold, persnickety, and pedantic while you are perceived as warm and easygoing, you will probably win the contract. Charm and quiet self-confidence are important qualities to enable you to be perceived in the right light, as is not upsetting people. If two Dominicans are in competition and their products are of equal merit, then the better connected of the two is likely to succeed. While having good connections is also important for foreigners, if two foreigners with equal merit are in competition, it is likely that the more charming one will clinch the deal.

Remember the Extended Family

One American executive working for a large Dominican company found that the single most important thing to remember, along with the importance of the family, is that everyone appears to be related to someone else. "Be careful who you call an idiot," he advised!

Doing favors and collecting favors owed is a highly developed art form in the DR—think of it as practical business insurance. These can be small kindnesses: if the director's wife, for example, has a physical complaint that you know responds to a natural product not available in the

DR, you might want to bring some with you and arrange to send more after you have left. It is worth doing some research into the Dominican company's owners and their likes, dislikes, and lifestyles.

Hierarchy and Respect

Name-dropping is commonplace and, as we have seen, nepotism does not raise eyebrows as it would in many other countries. The foreign businessperson also needs to pay attention to the hierarchy and show appropriate deference and respect to those in positions of authority. It is particularly important that the foreigner does nothing to cause a Dominican to lose face; the result is likely to be machismo rearing its head, and no deal. Dominicans can be very direct communicators and are not afraid to say what they feel; for the foreigner sometimes it is best to pause before responding and/or to know when to remain thoughtfully silent. It isn't a points scoring contest!

DRESS CODE

Appearances matter in the DR, and this applies at all levels of society. There is even a dress code for entering government offices—despite the heat, shorts and sandals are not permitted. Businesspeople are expected to dress well, but conservatively. Men should wear good-quality, dark-colored

business suits; sometimes the traditional *chacabana*, a white shirt worn over dark trousers, might be worn for formal meetings, particularly by older men. Women should dress elegantly, wearing stylish suits or dresses. Foreign visitors may request permission to remove their jackets in the high temperatures of the summer months, although many offices have effective air-conditioning that renders this unnecessary.

Hairstyles

Male hairstyles in the DR are short compared with some other countries; while long hair is tolerated in artistic and musical circles, it is definitely not the norm. Visible tattoos or body piercings are deemed inappropriate, and scrupulously clean shoes, fingernails, and teeth are expected. Dominicans take manicuring seriously, and even males might sport a thin coat of colorless varnish. This has absolutely no bearing on their gender orientation.

Women business entrepreneurs would be expected to wear elegant makeup and jewelry. Lipstick is noticeable here by European standards, but heavily designed, overlong false fingernails would give a misleading impression.

SETTING UP A MEETING

For large companies and multinationals, business appointments should be made in advance by telephone, e-mail, or fax. For smaller companies, appointments can be made by telephone.

> **Call the Day Before**
> *Inevitably, having arranged a meeting, you will be*
> *told, "Call me the day before to confirm." This can*
> *be disconcerting for foreigners because it sounds as*
> *if the final decision about the meeting will not be*
> *made until the day before, or as if the person has a*
> *bad memory or does not use a diary. While there*
> *could be some residual truth to all of these, if you*
> *remember "Si Dios quiere," you will recall the*
> *multitude of obstacles that can alter circumstances*
> *in a developing nation.*

It is certainly possible to make appointments
at short notice in the DR. The unsettling aspect
of this for the foreign entrepreneur is that it
will also be assumed that *you* are available for
meetings at short notice. In smaller companies
on the north coast it is still acceptable to "show
up" without an appointment to see if a contact
is there, particularly if your intermediary is a
friend of the person you want to see—and to
show up again the next day because the contact
was not there on the first try.

Time Keeping

The foreign businessperson should arrive on time
for the meeting, even if no one else does, but
there is absolutely no need to show up early. It is
important not to let the lateness of others unsettle
you, because it is something you will certainly
need to get used to.

MEETINGS

The first meeting is often quite formal and is as much to do with sizing up the foreigner as examining his product. Dominicans, who are extremely courteous, are very quick to sense unwarranted overfamiliarity, and can construe this as disrespect. It is usual for the meeting to begin with small talk in order to establish a rapport; you will not be expected to get down to business right away

How you react to what is "normal" in Dominican business meetings will determine your future success. Interruptions are to be expected, either via cell phone or in person, and several people may speak at the same time. Allow for this and take it in stride. It is helpful to have all your written materials available in both Spanish and English; likewise, if you have prearranged the use of an overhead projector for your presentation, text on slides should also be translated.

Expect Interruptions

Once you have started your presentation it will be normal for others to continue to arrive. Do not expect them to slip quietly in at the back—the small talk and questions about the health of family members will begin again. It helps if foreign entrepreneurs are laid-back about this and do not react like a coiled spring!

Keep your Cool!

The most important qualities to have are
flexibility and patience. It might be necessary to
deviate from your planned presentation in the
light of the managing director being called
elsewhere, a power outage rendering your visual
aids inoperable, or a multitude of other reasons.
Remember to control your facial expressions.
People in the DR are very aware of gestures and
body language. Always maintain good eye contact
with the person you are addressing; failure to do
so may be interpreted as losing interest in the
conversation. Be sure to appreciate the managing
director's sense of humor and don't try to "top"
him with one of your own jokes. The feathers of
machismo could get ruffled if you do.

Using Machismo to Advantage

What machismo will *allow you to do, if you are male, is
to gaze appreciatively at the secretary who brings in the
refreshments (as long as it isn't the managing director's
daughter, in a small company, so do your homework!).
Foreign women entrepreneurs are not advised to employ
the female equivalent of this tactic.*

NEGOTIATIONS

Expect the process to take longer than you are
used to. Agreement will not be reached until after
several meetings; negotiation and time for

consultation are important. Even if the people whom you are meeting seem all in favor of an idea or deal, there will always be someone else (mysteriously not present!) who has to be consulted. Dominicans are skilled negotiators and drive hard bargains, and they are well aware that it is easy to wear a foreigner down by replication of delays. If you try high-pressure sales tactics you could be seen as insulting people's intelligence, and if you try to rush the process you will be thought both rude and aggressive.

The Dominican entrepreneur will expect his foreign counterpart to set a high price and work downward. Dominicans at all levels of society *love* to negotiate, from the sale of tourist items to the purchasing of heavy machinery; it is not a good idea to rob them of this opportunity by setting your actual price from the start. How you handle the ongoing and time-consuming negotiation will be noticed; if you can enter into the fun of the negotiation, using good humor and patience and acknowledging the convincing nature of the other person's argument, Dominicans' respect for you will increase.

Most of the time negotiation is affable, but it can appear confrontational if you do not speak the language. It might look and sound as if the Dominicans around the table are having an argument, when all they are doing is debating animatedly and with exuberance. Since just about everything in the DR is done with exuberance, this should come as no surprise, but it does point to the need to have a good translator who is aware of your culture and any misunderstandings you might be construing. Higher-level staff speak excellent English in many of the multinational corporations, but the foreigner should not assume that this is the language which will be used, although he or she can request this.

CONTRACTS AND MINUTES

Since relationships are viewed as more important than business documents, it follows that minutes of meetings are not the norm in the DR. It is always possible for you to write a follow-up e-mail outlining the decisions arrived at; this would certainly be acceptable practice in the larger corporations, but the smaller, family businesses might view it with suspicion.

Contracts *are* an established procedure in the DR, and are drawn up by lawyers. In practice there seem to be no issues about deviating from the written contract, providing both parties are in agreement with the deviation. Should it ever come to litigation over contractual issues, however, you can count on the fact that every phrase therein will be punctiliously examined by your adversary's lawyers.

Frequently in the DR it is necessary to prompt or remind people of actions they agreed to take; follow-up should not be left to chance, nor should it take the form of nagging. There is a fine line between what expatriates who live here call "sitting on" people and being perceived as a colonialist imperialist oppressor. The secret is to follow up with a lot of charm and almost as if it were an afterthought, following discussion of other subjects. That way you will not be perceived as pointing out someone else's shortcomings or making them lose face.

MANAGEMENT STYLE

If you are not the ultimate authority in your company and you happen to upset someone, you might be surprised that your boss gets to hear about this before you do. To the first-world entrepreneur this might seem like telling tales out of school, but it is perfectly congruent with a highly stratified society in which autocratic management styles are the norm. This even applies to the Dominican community in New York City, so it is pretty deep-seated and unlikely to alter radically any time soon. This has implications for the foreign businessperson or entrepreneur who might be tasked with setting up a branch of his company in the DR—they will both need to and be expected to supervise staff more closely than they would at home. This is partly because of the relatively low standard of education in the DR, but also because "bosses are expected to be bosses." These can be tricky waters to navigate for the foreign manager determined not to be an imperialist oppressor, but it should be remembered that too egalitarian a management style will be perceived as weakness.

Staff are unlikely to bring a problem or issue to you for resolution. They will chat with coworkers, however, so you could get to hear of it this way. Sometimes "hypothetical" cases will be presented to the foreign manager. Preoccupied with both running the business and learning about the new culture, he or she may miss the point and could even misinterpret this as time wasting by staff. If this happens to you, stop and think again: chances are that a *real* problem is being presented in a hypothetical manner, and dealing with it today could save you hours of frustration in the future.

GIFTS AND BRIBERY

Small, inexpensive gifts in the business environment are acceptable, but proffering of expensive items very early in the relationship could engender suspicion. As we have seen, doing and calling in favors is a national art form, and it could be thought that a preemptory large-ticket item is a bribe. Small, personal gifts that show care and thought for the receiver are likely to be better received.

> **Gifts that Boost Status**
> *One of the most resounding successes I had was when I presented a prominent businessman with a personal business card case, the sort that is slipped into the trouser pocket. Card cases like that were not in common vogue in the DR at the time and Dominicans love being trendsetters, and said businessman could later be seen flashing his case around at every conceivable opportunity—plus a few inconceivable ones.* (GB)

If the foreign businessman gives items of this sort with his own company logo engraved on them, this would be seen as a promotion rather than a gift, but is equally acceptable.

It might seem strange to warn people away from lavish gift giving in such a clientelist society, but independent businesses do not necessarily operate in the same way that the government does, and for the foreigner it is better to rely on caution to avoid giving offense.

Government Agencies
If your business is with a government agency, you can pretty much rely on the fact that corruption is endemic. The *macuteo* (extortion) will make itself apparent way before you get to the person you want to see. There will be a number of intermediaries or brokers who will "facilitate" that journey, for a consideration. One large foreign

enterprise that had already invested upward of US $10 million in the DR went by appointment to discuss setting up another location for its business. The company's representatives  found that before they could get to the person they were meant to be meeting, they needed to "discuss" matters with a functionary in a gatekeeper position who was primarily interested in discussing his rake-off. They decided to leave, returned to the airport, and let everyone know what had happened.

There have been many attempts to combat corruption and the government has set up agencies specifically for this purpose, although it has not given them much in the way of powers to enforce. While their efforts might look good on paper, there is still a wide gulf between stated policy and actual practice.

chapter nine

COMMUNICATING

LANGUAGE

Dominican Spanish is fairly typical of the Spanish spoken in the rest of the Caribbean region. It is spoken fast and the ends of the words tend to be slurred, with -*ado* endings pronounced as "ao" and the letter "s" often disappearing completely, so a word like *pescados* (fish) can sound like "pecao" in a Dominican accent.

The most famous regional variation within the DR is the way the "r" is pronounced as an "l" in the capital, which is reversed in the southwest, and the "r" is pronounced as an "i" in the Cibao region, so the word *perdon* is "peldon" in the capital and "peidon" in the Cibao. In the south, the word *capital* may be pronounced as "capitarr."

Dominicanismos

When it comes to vocabulary, Dominican Spanish is standard Latin American Spanish (as opposed to Iberian Spanish) with some unique features.

Words and expressions derived from Taíno
Areito—ceremony
Batey—originally communal area of village, now cane-cutter settlement
Bohío—house
Casabe—cassava bread
Conuco—small vegetable plot

Words of African origin
Bemba—mouth
Guineo—banana
Mondongo—stew

Words that derive from English
Crinchí—cream cheese (*queso crema* is a country cheese)
Greifru—grapefruit (standard Spanish is *toronja* or *pomelo*)
Jonrón—home run (baseball)
Pana—friend, partner
Pariguayo—socially inept person (said to derive from "party watcher")
Play—baseball pitch
Poloché—polo shirt/T-shirt
Suape—mop (said to derive from "swab")
Zafacón—garbage can (said to derive from "safety can")

Words that derive from French
Caché—cachet, style

Words that derive from Italian
¡Eco lecuá!—That's right! Exactly!

In common with other Latin American Spanish dialects, Dominicans do not use the informal second-person plural *vosotros* form—*ustedes* is used in all cases.

Spanish is generally an easy language to learn, but even for an experienced Spanish speaker, or a native Spanish speaker from another country, the Dominican accent takes some getting used to. People will often slow down their pace and enunciate more clearly for a foreigner's benefit, but not always!

Words to Watch Out for

Some Spanish words that are innocent in other countries may take on a different meaning in the DR. One example is the word *culo*, which in Spain just means backside and is not a rude word, but is considered very crude in Dominican Spanish. Dominicans and many other Latin Americans say *nalga* or *trasero* to refer to the posterior in polite company.

In any Spanish-speaking country, words that sound like their English equivalent may mean something rather different. "Embarrassed" is not *embarazada*—this means "pregnant"—and you don't "introduce," you "present," because *introducir* means to insert.

Some foods have different names in the DR: bananas are called *guineo*, goat is called *chivo*, and oranges are sometimes called *china*.

Other languages spoken in the DR include English by educated Dominicans and those who have lived in the USA. Haitian Creole, or Kreyol, is widely spoken by Haitian migrants but also by some Dominicans in the areas along the border. German, Italian, and French, together with English, are spoken by people working in the tourist areas.

ETIQUETTE

In the DR, it's not so much what you say as how you phrase it that counts. People do not say please and thank you as much as English speakers, and do not expect to hear it as frequently. A respectful, courteous approach preceded by a greeting is expected, and is considered far more important.

People don't just approach strangers and launch into a request: they always start off by saying "*Buenos días*," "*Buenas tardes*," "*Buenas noches*," or just "*Buenas*," "*Saludos*," or even "*Hola*." A young person can be addressed as *joven* (both sexes), *señorita* (young woman), or *amigo/a*. A child could be *amiguito/a*. An older person should be addressed as *Señor* or *Señora*, *Don* or *Doña*.

When entering a waiting room, elevator, small shop, or restaurant, getting on a bus, or in a public car, one should make a general greeting, usually "*Saludos*" or "*Buenas*." When approaching a person who is eating, people say "*Buen provecho*." If you are eating and someone comes into the room, you should say "*A buen tiempo*." Upon leaving a restaurant it is customary to say "*Buen provecho*" to people still eating their meals.

With strangers, except perhaps with little children, the polite form of "you"—*usted*—should be used, as opposed to the informal *tú*.

Greetings in both informal and formal settings are more ritualized than visitors may be used to. When faced with a group of people you are expected to greet every person individually, introducing yourself and saying "*Un placer*" ("A pleasure"), "*Encantado/a*," or "*Mucho gusto*" ("Pleased to meet you"). Women kiss each other once on the right cheek. Women greeting men may or may not offer their cheeks for a kiss—it depends how well they know each other and on the situation. If you do not feel comfortable doing this, it is fine to shake hands instead. Men shake hands with each other, and if they are friends they will engage in a brief hug and shoulder pat.

BODY LANGUAGE

One of the most typical Dominican gestures is pointing with the lips: the lips are pursed and the head is jerked in the direction of the indicated person or object. It can also be used as a gesture of frustration or disapproval.

A wrinkle of the nose is often shorthand for "I didn't quite catch that—please repeat it."

Finger wagging is a way of saying "no"; fanning the index finger from side to side is an acceptable way of rejecting a street vendor or traffic-light car window cleaner.

There is also an index finger circular movement to indicate "later"—or, in good

Dominican Spanish, *ahorita*, which is like *mañana* but without the same sense of urgency.

The familiar middle-finger salute has the same meaning in the DR. It is used to great effect as a form of communication between drivers.

Don't Take It Personally!

Like other Latins, Dominicans will remark on aspects of your physical appearance with shocking frankness. They may well call you *grandote/a* or *gordo/a* if you are heavily built and "*flaco/a*" if you are slim. This is merely an affectionate statement of fact, and bear in mind that to be called "fat" is considered a compliment, especially among older people, who still associate fat with health and prosperity and slimness with poverty and disease.

Note also that *rubio/a* does not mean blond/e in the strictest sense: any white person, even a dark-haired, dark-eyed one, is included in this category. While *moreno/a* means brunette in Spain, in the DR it is reserved for the darkest-skinned black people. *Negro* for black is never used—it is considered derogatory. It is likely that Dominican Miss Universe 2003 was taken aback at being described in the Spanish press as "*morena*" for this reason. With dark brown hair, brown eyes, and white skin, she is very much a *rubia* in her own country. In contrast, as a Mediterranean-featured brunette, it took me a while to realize that people meant me when they called out "*Rubia!*" in the street. (IB)

PDAs not Welcome

Somewhat surprisingly for such a sensuous, spontaneous, and affectionate culture, public displays of affection between lovers are unacceptable for straight and gay couples alike. You rarely see couples walking along with their arms around each other, let alone kissing in the street as in Europe, for example. On the other hand, young women friends especially will walk arm in arm or hand in hand with each other, and men are also much more physically affectionate with each other compared to northern European and North American men.

HUMOR

The Dominican sense of humor is lively and direct. People enjoy teasing, a certain degree of gentle ribbing, and banter. Puns and wordplay are big favorites, although much of this will go over the heads of the non-Spanish speaker. In films and TV comedy shows humor is mainly of the slapstick variety, and the concept of political correctness doesn't come into it.

THE MEDIA

In a country where press freedom is a fluid concept, and the open persecution of journalists like Orlando Martínez and Narciso González is still fresh in the collective memory (even fresher since the decision of the Inter American Commision on Human Rights in May 2010 to sue the DR in the case of the latter), it is surprising that some journalists, most notably Huchi Lora and Nuria Piera, can be bold and outspoken, tackling taboo subjects such as government corruption head-on. At the same time, the mainstream media outlets are largely submissive to the status quo—most are owned by powerful banking families and many depend on government advertising revenue for their survival.

Television

All the main TV channels apart from four are private. There are a couple of dozen other privately owned national and regional channels. The usual selection of international channels is available via cable and satellite; the main providers are Aster, Telecable (cable), and Sky (satellite). The advent of international cable and satellite television has marginalized Dominican television to some extent, but political talk shows and popular entertainment programs are still watched by millions.

MAIN NATIONAL TV CHANNELS	
2	Teleantillas
4	CERTV (state-run)
5	Telemicro
7	Antena Latina
9	Color Vision
13	Telecentro
37	CDN (Cadena de Noticias)

Radio

The radio still plays an important part in everyday life, in a country where much of communication is aural—this is for deep-seated cultural reasons and because a significant percentage of the population is illiterate or semiliterate. Popular radio talk shows like *El Gobierno de la Mañana* (*The Government of the Morning*) and Huchi Lora's afternoon show are outspoken and instrumental in shaping and influencing opinion. In rural areas, the Catholic Church has used community radio stations like Radio Enriquillo in the southwest and Radio Santa María to educate as well as inform and entertain people. Before the days of mass telephone ownership, stations like Radio Guarachita were important for keeping people in touch with their relatives in other parts of the country. Radio is also a popular medium for that other Dominican passion—music.

Newspapers

Dominican newspapers have a relatively low circulation and as online readership grows, this is set to decline even further. The main dailies are *Listín Diario*, *Diario Libre* (free), *Hoy*, *El Caribe*, *El Día* (free), *El Nacional*, and *El Nuevo Diario*. There is also a weekly paper called *CLAVE*. There are no print newspapers in English since the *Santo Domingo News* stopped printing in the late 1990s.

Internet

The main newspapers all have Web sites, and the weekly *CLAVE* has a daily online sister publication known as *Clave Digital*. Several new online newspapers have sprung up, as well as a healthy blogosphere. There are several English-language news resources, the main ones being DR1, which publishes a daily news digest on weekdays, and *Dominican Today*, which publishes quick translations of the main news stories six days a week. Internet use is growing, with 415,000 accounts or more than three million people with access to the World Wide Web—in Latin America and the Caribbean, the DR ranks sixth in terms of Internet penetration (26.9 percent). The main telecommunications companies are Codetel/Claro, Orange Dominicana, Tricom, and Viva.

Telephones

In 2010, the DR had over 9.5 million telephones for a population of over 9.5 million inhabitants—100 percent coverage. Just 9.9 percent of the population has a landline, while 86.7 percent have cellular phones. Cell phone use has revolutionized communications, especially for poor Dominicans.

Mail

The Dominican postal system is not considered reliable, and people tend to use private national and international alternatives. Within towns and cities motorbike messengers are used to send and receive correspondence, bills, and statements. Between cities the main bus companies Metro and Caribe Tours have efficient and inexpensive courier services. For international mail, several companies provide a PO box address in Miami and a courier service to and from the DR.

CONCLUSION

We hope we have provided something of a roadmap to the interesting and challenging experiences that await you in the Dominican Republic. You could choose to spend a couple of weeks vegetating deep within the confines of an all-inclusive tourist resort, but we hope you won't. The memories you take back with you will be greatly enhanced by getting out and meeting the Dominican people and understanding their different lifestyles. If you are concerned that their immediacy, warmth, vitality, and contradictions might be too overwhelming to take in on one visit, you may be tempted to make two or three— or to do what the authors did, and make this country your home.

Further Reading

Alvarez, Julia. *In the Time of the Butterflies*. New York: Plume Books, 1995.

Bedggood, Ginnie. *Quisqueya: Mad Dogs And English Couple*. Best Books Online, 2007. Now out of print. Available online at:
http://www.offshorewave.com/Moving_To_The_Dominican_Republic.htm

Candelario, Ginetta. *Black behind the Ears: Dominican Racial Identity from Museums to Beauty Shops*. Durham and London: Duke University Press, 2007.

CIA "Family Jewels" memo, 1973. Available at
http://www.gwu.edu/~nsarchiv/NSAEBB/NSAEBB222/family_jewels_full_ocr.pdf

Díaz, Junot. *The Brief Wondrous Life Of Oscar Wao*. New York: Riverhead, 2008.

Gonzalez, Clara and Ilana Benady. *Aunt Clara's Dominican Cookbook*. Santo Domingo: Lunch Club Press, 2007.

Keefer, Philip. *Clientelism, Credibility and the Policy Choices of Young Democracies*. Washington, DC: World Bank Development Research Group, 2005.

Moya Pons, Frank. *The Dominican Republic: A National History*, 2nd ed. New Rochelle, NY: Markus Wiener, 1998.

Pollock, David and Ruth Van Reken. *Third Culture Kids: Growing Up Among Worlds*. Boston and London: Nicholas Brealey Publishing, 2009.

Sagás, Ernesto. "A Case of Mistaken Identity: Antihaitianismo in Dominican Culture." *Latinamericanist* 29 (1), 1993. Available at
http://www.webster.edu/~corbetre/haiti/misctopic/dominican/conception.htm

Soong, Roland. *Racial Classifications in Latin America*. 1999. Available at
www.zonalatina.com/Zldata55.htm.

Torres-Saillant, Silvio. "The Tribulations of Blackness: Stages in Dominican Racial Identity." *Latin American Perspectives* 25 (3), 1998.

UNDP *Human Development Report*, 2008. Available at
www.pnud.org.do/sites/pnud.onu.org.do/files/Resumen_Ingles.pdf.

US Bureau of Democracy, Human Rights and Labor (DRL). 2009 *Human Rights Report: Dominican Republic*. DRL, March 11th 2010. Available at
http://www.state.gov/g/drl/rls/hrrpt/2009/wha/136110.htm

Wucker, Michelle. *Why the Cocks Fight: Dominicans, Haitians, and the Struggle for Hispaniola*. New York: Hill & Wang, 2000.

Useful Web Sites

www.pages.drexel.edu/~sd65/carib_history/arawaks.htm
Arawak and Taíno history.

www.dominicancooking.com

www.ginniebedggood.com

www.santeriareligion101.com

www.one.gob.do
DR statistics. ENHOGAR 2005, DR National Statistics Office (ONE)

www.dr1.com

culture smart! **dominican republic**

Index